Heartfelt Inspirations

Heartfelt Inspirations

Devotions from the Christian Authors Guild

Compiled and Edited by
Diana J. Baker

© 2008 by Diana J. Baker. All rights reserved.

Pleasant Word (a division of WinePress Publishing, PO Box 428, Enumclaw, WA 98022) functions only as book publisher. As such, the ultimate design, content, editorial accuracy, and views expressed or implied in this work are those of the author.

No part of this publication may be reproduced, stored in a retrieval system or transmitted in any way by any means—electronic, mechanical, photocopy, recording or otherwise—without the prior permission of the copyright holder, except as provided by USA copyright law.

The author of this book has waived the publisher's suggested editing and proof reading services. As such, the author is responsible for any errors found in this finished product.

Unless otherwise noted, all scripture references are taken from the *Authorized King James Version* of the Bible.

ISBN 13: 978-1-4141-1220-6
ISBN 10: 1-4141-1220-3
Library of Congress Catalog Card Number: 2008902924

Contents

Preface xi

Building Materials 1
Visiting the Hortons 2
Mailbox Turtle 3
Eyewitnesses 4
Answered Prayer 5
A New Song 6
The Third Cry 7
Be Strong–Do Exploits 8
The Nose of the Camel 9
Gird Up the Loins of Your Mind 10
Dispelling Darkness 11
Do Good Things 12
Blind Spots 13
Big Events 14
A Good Name 15
Tender Hearts 16
Food for the Mind 17
Creator of Heaven and Earth 18
Pillar of Flowers 19
An Empty Cupboard Filled 20
You Are Not Alone 21
The Mighty Fortress: A Person 22
Better Than an Instant Message 23
Daily Renewal 24
My He-man 25
New Beginnings 26
Building Bigger Barns 27

The Hand of God	28
How Much Do You Weigh?	29
Bear One Another's Burdens	30
Proving Our Love	31
A New Song to Sing	32
Relationship With God	33
A New Creature	34
My Joyful Noise	35
Equal Spoils	36
Problem Solver	37
The Hiding Place	38
The Joy of Giving	39
Really Giving	40
Ravens on Assignment	41
Fearfully and Wonderfully Made	42
A Tree Falls in the Forest	43
Spiritual Battle	44
Jesus Knows My Name	45
Hearing Moses and the Prophets	46
Missing Keys—Lost or Misplaced?	47
Sequestered in Silence	48
Pictures of Love	49
Angels Among Us	50
Confident Prayer	51
Assurance of Tomorrow	52
Talk to Me	53
Consistency or Predictability?	54
The Greatest Gift	55
It is Well	56
Station Yourselves	57
The Value of Prayer	58
Remember Me	59
Small Things Can Make All the Difference	60
A Moment in Time	61
Don't Let Go of the Word	62
Quiet Time?	63
Hill Street Blues	64

The Lord's Unexpected Return	65
Sunday Dinner	66
Encounters of the Personal Kind	67
A Jot or a Tittle	68
Springs of Living Water	69
You Need a Friend	70
We Are Sojourners	71
Unseen Protection	72
Higher Learning	73
Never Fear Bad News	74
Beautiful Flight—No Landing Gear	75
When the Rain Falls, the Creeks Rise	76
Where Are You?	77
What'll You Have?	78
Stand Fast in Your Liberty	79
The View From Within	80
The Glory of His Light	81
Oh, Happy Day	82
Dialing 9-1-1…Answering 9-1-1	83
Hope	84
Freedom of Choice	85
Gramps	86
Moses: Servant of God and Psalm Writer	87
The Guiding Candle	88
Knowledge and Freedom	89
Words of Life	90
Desires of Your Heart	91
Growing Through Temptation	92
Finding Your Purpose	93
Lift One Another Up	94
Keep, Kept, Cooped?	95
Carved in the Palm of His Hand	96
The Problem of Patience	97
Father of Lies	98
Needs Met	99
Wrinkles, Worry, and Sin	100
Next Someday	101

Facing Hard Times	102
Love is the Greatest	103
God Doesn't Make Junk	104
Peace of Mind in Troubling Times	105
Hide the Word	106
Rainy Days, Mondays, and Certain Songs	107
Refuge and Stronghold	108
Plant Deep Roots	109
Good Enough—Just Not Perfect	110
What Stands in Our Way?	111
Our Word is Our Bond	112
Scalding to Balding	113
Possessing the Land	114
Disguised Manna	115
Holy Enough	116
Strange Can Be Good	117
Baggage	118
Refresh and Be Refreshed	119
For His Good Pleasure	120
The Christmas Tree Search	121
Take and Eat	122
Songs of Deliverance	123
His Eye is On the Sparrow	124
To Catch a Fly—Honey vs. Vinegar	125
Faithful Until the End	126
Watch Your Language	127
Teamwork	128
A Gentle Man	129
Unseen Answers	130
Standing in Faith	131
A Mother's Concern	132
Trust	133
Perfect Peace	134
What Do You Have in Your Hand?	135
An Anchor That Holds	136
A Tired Christian	137
In Times of Trouble: Rejoice!	138

The Prize	139
Fruit in the Wilderness	140
God's Candle	141
Not Being Rich Toward God	142
Twenty-Twenty Vision	143
God Is With Us	144
The Riches of Christ	145
Giving Up Habits	146
Casting Shadows or Light	147
Chariots of Fire	148
Remedy for Guilt	149
The Narrow Gate	150
Does Anyone Care?	151
What's Your Worth?	152
God's Wonderful Protection	153
The Great Commission	154
The Traveler	155
Jesus Lives	156
The Spiritually Healthy Heart	157
The Jesus I Knew	158
Personal Testimony	159
Wait on the Lord	160
Still Waters	161
Satan's Lies	162
God's Garden of Life	163
Winters	164
Change Your Thinking—Your Mind	165
Chipmunks	166
The Just Shall Live by Faith	167
The Repairer	168
Out of the Comfort Zone	169
She Did What She Could	170
Role Model	171
Beauty From Within	172
The Promise	173
The Worst Words	174
The Ripple Effect	175

Author and Finisher	176
Sing Praise	177
Who's Your Daddy?	178
Wait for God's Direction	179
A Man Who Pleased God	180
Whom Should We Fear?	181
The Unchanging Heart	182
The Power of Comfort	183
Seeing Clearly	184
This Little Light of Mine	185
The Power of Words	186
Light Your World	187
The Conviction of Courage	188
Widow's Weeds	189
The Path of the Just	190
Meet the Authors	191

Preface

Heartfelt Inspirations: Devotions from the Christian Authors Guild is the fourth book to be published by the Christian Authors Guild of Woodstock, Georgia. It follows a memoir book, *Stepping Stones across the Stream of Time* (2003), a book of short stories, *The Desk in the Attic* (2004), and a book of testimonies, *No Small Miracles* (2005).

Our desire in publishing this book is to inspire you, the reader, to allow the Holy Spirit to draw you closer to God and to His Son, the Lord Jesus Christ, as you read the truths revealed in God's Word and in the accounts of lives that have been changed by those truths.

The Christian Authors Guild was founded in April, 2000 by Cheryl Norwood through the inspiration of the Blue Ridge Mountains Christian Writers Conference. It was Cheryl's dream to create a local writers group to help writers improve their writing skills, share their Christian faith, encourage one another, and impact the world by touching lives—one reader at a time. She believed that writing was a gift to be used to wash like a Christian wave over the secular world. That belief became CAG's theme, "Sending out a Christian Wave upon a Secular Sea."

Members of the guild enjoy semimonthly meetings, which include writing-related teachings, exercises for improving writing skills, opportunities to share rejections and publishing successes, and fellowship. Members also benefit from CAG's web site, www.christianauthorsguild.org, its monthly online newsletter, *The Wave*, fiction and non-fiction critique groups, yearly conferences, publication in CAG books, and access to a lending library.

We thank you for allowing us to touch your life with our words. We pray that you will be richly blessed as God speaks to your heart through His Word and our heartfelt inspirations.

Diana J. Baker

Building Materials

By Susan M. Watkins

Bible Reading: Ecclesiastes 3:1-8

"A time to cast away stones, and a time to gather stones together."

—Ecclesiastes 3:5a

Collecting stones—the childhood pastime of compiling rock treasures, storing them in shoeboxes under unmade beds, and trading them with closest friends. Stones that never change form though their owners do.

David crouched into his destiny and selected five smooth stones from the riverbed. A giant taunted the God that David privately worshipped in song while tending his first flock. David's character towered above Goliath, minimizing his insults.

Nehemiah surveyed the fallen wall of Jerusalem. Stones broken and charred were evaluated for reconstruction. Nothing would be wasted—an echo of God's perception of broken lives. Driven by restoration; the useable, used.

The act of gathering stones ignites faith. David's simple exercise ultimately brought him before King Saul. Could he have imagined that such a simple gesture would grant him a king's audience? Never underestimate simple talents. They represent a purposeful gathering to follow a master plan and erect or level the edifice of God's design.

Christ's wisdom is best displayed in the public arena. Caught in an act of sin, a shamed woman is thrown at His feet. The equally guilty man disappears into the hardened crowd as stones are gathered for projectile verdicts. Christ surveys the granite hearts and tips the scales' weights. The sinless One, the Chief Cornerstone, penetrates walled minds and challenges the sinless to launch their judgments. Stones are briefly airborne on their downward journeys from guilty palms to dusty feet. All learn the lesson.

The gathering of stones results from motivations of the heart. Whether defending, rebuilding, or judging, care must be given in their collection and distribution. Gather your stones wisely.

Lord, help me see Your purpose before I act.

Visiting the Hortons

By Cheryl Anderson Davis

Bible Reading: I Timothy 4:14-16

"Or ever the silver cord be loosed…Then shall the dust return to the earth as it was: and the spirit shall return unto God who gave it."

—Ecclesiastes 12:6-7

A couple named Horton have a place at the end of the country road where I live. I visit the Hortons whenever I get weary of breaking up fights between my kids, discover that I forgot to pay the telephone bill, or feel exhausted after long hours at my job.

The Hortons never console me when life is not going my way. They never tell me if I am right or wrong. They let me figure a lot of things out on my own. In fact, the Hortons never say anything to me.

I respect their silence, because all that is left of the Hortons are two weather-worn tombstones in an overgrown graveyard. The Hortons died over a century ago and are buried in the churchyard of a church that no longer exists.

When I visit the Hortons, I remember that I, too, will one day be in the cold ground, and I am blessed with a new perspective on the importance of what is happening around me. I am reminded that life is very short, and that all those small dramas that so preoccupy my thoughts are nothing more than distractions. I realize those worldly problems are keeping me from doing God's will and from using the gifts I have been blessed with in this life.

Dear Lord, I pray that I will remember to use the gifts You have given me. Do not allow the petty troubles of this world to distract me from acting on Your will.

Mailbox Turtle

By Pam I. Barnes

Bible Reading: Deuteronomy 30:1-3

"And shalt return unto the Lord thy God, and shalt obey his voice according to all that I command thee this day, thou and thy children, with all thine heart, and with all thy soul."

—Deuteronomy 30:2

As a child, I was blessed to have many pets. I had dogs, cats, turtles, a skunk, and a horse. I learned many lessons from the care of my animals. I learned about love and responsibility and about discipline and obeying rules. Those lessons are still in my heart.

I learned one such lesson through an incident with my turtle, Charley. Mom had scolded me for riding Charley in my bicycle basket. I told her he enjoyed it, and she assured me he did not. I was told to never do it again, but I disobeyed.

One day while riding Charley around, I wanted to join some of my friends who were also riding bikes. To save time, I put Charley in my mailbox instead of returning him to his pen. I didn't want anything bad to happen to him or to lose him. My intentions were good.

The next afternoon, to her horror, my mother—who wasn't very fond of turtles—found poor Charley in the mailbox. Thank goodness he was still alive. The scolding she gave me for disobeying her and for putting Charley in danger helped me realize that good intentions did not always assure good decisions. I had to repent and ask for forgiveness.

Dear God, thank You for lessons in life and for trusting me to care for Your beautiful creatures. Thank You for loving and caring for me.

Eyewitnesses

By Cynthia L. Simmons

Bible Reading: II Peter 1:12-19

"For we have not followed cunningly devised fables, when we made known unto you the power and coming of our Lord Jesus Christ, but we were eyewitnesses of his majesty."

—II Peter 1:16

As Peter wrote those words, he knew he faced a martyr's death. Someone facing death wouldn't waste time discussing trivial things, and he didn't. The message in II Peter held vital truths he wanted believers to cling to. He had been a leader in the early church. He worried that after his death the church might forget what he had taught or that false teachers might deceive them.

Peter wrote to remind believers they had not believed a clever fairy tale. He testified that he had witnessed the spiritual world first-hand at the transfiguration. The glory of God had rested on Jesus, and Peter had seen the heavenly glow on His face. God had spoken from Heaven to proclaim that Jesus was His Son. Peter and the other apostles had preached a gospel straight from God.

At times, I get caught up in the mundane details of life. Miraculous Bible stories seem unreal, and I wonder if someone just made them up for fearful children. When I'm tempted to doubt, I remind myself of Peter's words. He saw into the spiritual world at the transfiguration. Afterward, he gave us a compelling eyewitness account. Later, he paid a price—his life—for his testimony. His faith inspires me to believe and to testify.

Lord, there are times I'm tempted to question the truth of Scripture. Help me cling to the testimony of those who saw your power displayed and gave their lives to declare it. Keep my faith strong and keep me from doubting Your Word.

Answered Prayer

By Charlene Elder

Bible Reading: Psalm 118:18-29

"I will praise thee: for thou hast heard me, and art become my salvation."
—Psalm 118:21

Jim and Bev were building their retirement home on the top of a North Georgia mountain when they encountered difficulty in locating water for a well. Several attempts to drill had been unsuccessful, and the building plans could not proceed until they had a well in place. They had not mentioned their need to anyone until my husband and I visited. After we had enjoyed their majestic mountain view and were preparing to leave, they asked for prayer. They desperately needed water—they needed a well.

We stood on the property hand-in-hand and prayed, asking for God's wisdom to direct the next well digger to locate water for their well. We prayed for an abundance of water. We agreed together for God's provision to be manifested, and then Jack and I drove home.

Less than a week later, Jim and Bev called to give us an awesome praise report: water had been found, the well was in place, and they would have more water than they could use in a lifetime. We rejoiced with them because God had abundantly answered our prayer.

Lord, help me always remember that You are interested in every aspect of my life, and You will answer my prayers. I will continue to praise and thank You for those answers.

A New Song

By M.L. Anderson

Bible Reading: Psalm 33:3

"Sing unto him a new song."

—Psalm 33:3a

Have you ever wondered if the Lord was calling you into full-time Christian ministry? I did. I agonized in the church pew every Sunday, trapped in middle age, middle management, and middle-class yuppie-ness. I longed for God to grant me boldness to break free and serve Him.

One morning in 1985, our pastor built a sermon around Psalm 33:3 and my heart erupted with excitement. Within months, I left the corporate regimentation, tore off my tie, and rolled up my sleeves for God.

Operating a ministry, especially a Christian enterprise, has its costs. In the months that followed, friends were critical and thought I was crazy for giving up my "real job." I watched as my household income plummeted, and it was in quiet moments during those hungry first years that I sometimes questioned my decision.

Serving our Lord has intangible rewards of the soul-soothing kind. The years I operated the New Song Christian Bookstores were the most fulfilling of my life. I felt totally alive. I grew keenly aware of my portion of His plan to disseminate truth by putting books, Bibles, and music into the hands of those who needed them. God brought many godly people through the doors of the stores, and I thank Him often for His calling on my heart, for the courage to step out in faith, and for the privilege of serving Him by serving others.

Thank You, Lord, for all the second chances, u-turns, and start-overs You allow me to take and make in my life. Help me never to be ungrateful for the new songs You give me.

The Third Cry

By Bill Larmore

Bible Reading: Matthew 26:69-75

"Then began he to curse and to swear, *saying*, I know not the man. And immediately the cock crew. And Peter remembered the word of Jesus, which said unto him, Before the cock crow, thou shalt deny me thrice. And he went out, and wept bitterly."

—Matthew 26:74-75

While Jesus prayed, Peter and the other apostles—their bellies comfortably full from their Passover dinner—were drowsing quietly in the warm, fragrant, moonlit gloom of the Garden of Gethsemane. Peter was on the defensive because his beloved master had challenged His disciples by speaking these words, "All ye shall be offended because of me this night." When he had heard Jesus' words, Peter had immediately declared that despite cowardice of lesser men, he would stand firm for Jesus. He had boomed out, "Though all men shall be offended because of thee, yet will I never be offended."

Jesus' response, "Verily I say unto thee that this night, before the cock crow, thou shalt deny me thrice," had struck the big fisherman like a clenched fist. Peter had confidently answered, "Though I should die with thee, yet will I not deny thee."

Our scripture focus tells the rest of the sad story—Jesus had spoken truth. Each of us could exchange Peter's name for ours. I pray that we will never place confidence in our own strength. Peter's yesterdays form memorable lessons for our Christian tomorrows.

Dear Father in Heaven, help me see the wisdom and necessity of looking beyond myself to You alone for support and assistance. Please teach me to never hold too high an opinion of my own constancy in the hour of temptation.

BE STRONG–DO EXPLOITS

By Jack G. Elder

Bible Reading: I Thessalonians 5:23-24

"…but the people that do know their God shall be strong, and do *exploits*."
—Daniel 11:32b

When we hear the word "exploits" we think of explorers searching out new lands, like the famous Lewis and Clark searching for a passageway to the Pacific Ocean. Or in more current days, we might think of astronauts traveling to the moon or setting up space stations. Some think of exploits in sports and those who are setting new records and reaching beyond what others have done.

Exploits are daring and notable feats. That definition seems to fit men like Martin Luther, John Wesley, and Billy Graham. That list leaves us with the daunting thought, *how can the average Christian do daring deeds and feats like the great men of God did?*

We live in a society where even the smallest deed as a Christian takes courage. It requires people who first, know their God and second, stand strong in that knowledge. We find knowledge in the Word and the joy of learning brings strength to obey it.

We have the same God as the great men and women of faith—the great cloud of witnesses. We can do even greater things. Doing great things for God is simply doing what He asks us to do. Whatever that is—do it.

Father, help me do exploits in Your name and for Your name's sake. In myself, I know I don't have the ability. Help me to be strong and do what You ask me to do in Your strength.

The Nose of the Camel

By June Parks

Bible Reading: Matthew 19:24; Mark 10:25; Luke 18:25

"For it is easier for a camel to go through a needle's eye, than for a rich man to enter into the kingdom of God."

—Luke 18:25

A famous joke tells of a camel hiding by sticking his nose inside a tent. He thought he couldn't be seen. Of course, the biggest part of the camel was left out, but the most important part was where it counted. His nosey nose was inside the tent, and his thinking part was where it needed to be.

Be aware; the whole world could be looking. Most people are seeing our "hanging out" part. There's no way to hide. Our lives are judged by what people see. Even though we hide our eyes, our actions are "hanging out."

Most importantly, our Lord knows if we are hiding anything. If we're trying to hide our actions—He knows; our thoughts—He knows; our fortunes—He knows. Beware of all of that. That ugly camel stands a better chance of getting through the eye of a needle than the rich have trying to hold on to their riches and slip through into the kingdom of God.

We cannot take our riches with us. That old camel would stand a better chance of getting through. And we want to get through.

Dear Lord, help me know that the big, old camel in scripture is an example to encourage me to do what I have to do to attain the kingdom of heaven. Please keep me and help me be a good example when I am "hanging out there."

Gird Up the Loins of Your Mind

By Patty Rocco

Bible Reading: I Peter 1

"Wherefore gird up the loins of your mind, be sober, and hope to the end for the grace that is to be brought unto you at the revelation of Jesus Christ."

—I Peter 1:13

Many times we can find spiritual truth in movies. Recently, I heard a film character warn his colleagues to "gird your loins," because the boss was unexpectedly on her way. The phrase caused me to open the Word and ponder what Peter meant by 'gird up the loins of your mind.'

Like Peter, I've stumbled at trusting Christ while circumstances were bleak. I've taken matters into my own hands, while Christ called to me from the shore. Since Peter learned to gird up the loins of his mind through many severe trials, I, too, have hope that I can become more intimate with the standards of God if I choose to "gird up the loins of my mind."

In the previously mentioned movie, the employees worked by different standards. When the boss was away, they worked by another standard than when she was present. Our heavenly Father wants me to always work and play by His standard, the Word of God. He asks me to be holy. It is a high calling, but He gives me the Spirit and the Word to guide me each day.

Father, I thank You for the standard set forth in Your Word. Thank You for the shed blood of Christ that allows me to enter into a relationship that pursues that standard. Thank You for the Holy Spirit, who dwells within me and reminds me when I've missed Your best and offers Your forgiveness and peace when I ask for it.

Dispelling Darkness

By Susan M. Watkins

Bible Reading: Luke 15:8-10

"Either what woman having ten pieces of silver, if she lose one piece, doth not light a candle, and sweep the house, and seek diligently till she find it?"

—Luke 15:8

Finding a lost coin required light. The woman in this parable knew her abilities were impeded in the dark. She was industrious and possessed the wisdom to succeed in her endeavor, although sweeping and thoroughly searching would require illumination.

We are called to be the light of the world—a simple definition defying the depths of explanation. Light is an amazing property. A single lit match can be seen from an airplane at 30,000 feet. One match!

If you walk down a dark hallway and enter a well-lit room, the hallway's darkness does not flood into the lit room. Rather, the light through the room's open door bathes the darkened hall. God has commissioned each of us to be His light and a beacon to the internally veiled.

Light has within itself the property to expose slippery roads and keep us from danger. It is a righteous, internal governor that directs our steps. With the right tools, we are assured of success. We might need to recalibrate our mindset to dispose of our bushel baskets so we can visibly shine as examples for those around us.

This parable promises acquisition. After combining light, effort, and Olympic determination, the woman is crowned the victor. She promptly announces that God's way of solving problems is always victorious. Joyful celebration ensues.

If there is no light on our horizon, we must carry God's light to it. He can faithfully interpret obscured areas in our lives. He did, after all…ignite the sun!

Lord, light my life and heart and draw others to You through my example.

Do Good Things

By Joan Duvall

Bible Reading: Luke 6:27-38

"And as ye would that men should do to you, do ye also to them likewise."
—Luke 6:31

I went into the break room at work and noticed the microwave was dirty. I thought *no one ever cleans it.* Then God said, "Why don't you clean it?"

I thought about it for a moment. I didn't want to clean the microwave. I had not made the mess. However, I began to clean it anyway—for God.

The cleaning lady came into the room after I had finished and was washing off the sink. She appeared tired and didn't say a word. I understood that God had been showing me an example of doing a good deed. I had just received a lesson on kindness. The lesson: if I could get past myself, I could be a blessing to others.

After seeing the lady's load lifted a bit, I felt good. Even though it required a little effort from me, it made me realize it was a nice thing to do. The knowledge impressed on my heart that day was something valuable from God concerning life: that it is not always about me, but about someone else too. God's lesson on kindness had given me my reward.

Thank You, Lord, for showing me how to be kind to others without expecting anything in return. And thank You for allowing me to recognize that helping others is the right thing to do and demonstrates Your unconditional love and compassion. I now understand Your Golden Rule for kingdom living better.

Blind Spots

By Margaret Fagre

Bible Reading: Luke 15:11-32

"And when he came to himself, he said, How many hired servants of my father's have bread enough and to spare, and I perish with hunger! I will arise and go to my father, and will say unto him, Father, I have sinned against heaven and before thee."

—Luke 15:17-18

The prodigal son should have had a physical before he left his home. His ears were not working normally, because he could not hear the words of wisdom that his father spoke. His eyes were defective, because he could not see very far down the road. He had a blind spot in his thinking, because he did not know the truth about life—that true joy and happiness are found in family and in the love of God.

I can relate to blind spots. When I am driving and need to change lanes, I have to pay close attention to possible blind spots. I need to be alert with my eyes, so I can see all of the other cars clearly.

I think the prodigal son had his vision blocked by the lusts of this world. When all the pleasures faded, he could then see clearly to repent. When he came to himself, he had ears that could hear and eyes that could see. His mind had clarity—no more blind spots—and he could see things as they really were. When he stopped focusing on his selfish desires, his father's house came back into his line of vision.

Father, I am grateful for the story of the prodigal son. Help me have ears that can hear the Holy Spirit and eyes that can see into eternity.

BIG EVENTS

By Robert W. Ellis

Bible Reading: John 10:7-10

"The thief cometh not, but for to steal, and to kill, and to destroy: I am come that they might have life, and that they might have it more abundantly."

—John 10:10

Our lives are shaped by many events. Some events are small and seemingly insignificant; others are big, and we live with the memory of them for the rest of our days. If you ask people what they were doing on September 11, 2001, most can tell you in minute detail.

In some cases, there are personal events in our own lives that haunt us and cause us great despair. Those were events that we had a part in that were harmful to us or to others, and we cannot change or erase them. Those events often changed our personalities and our relationships with other people.

It is only when we realize that God forgives and comforts His children with unrestrained love that we are able to move past those events and move on with our lives and relationships. God only wants us to come to Him and seek His forgiveness.

Another set of big events that happened over two thousand years ago make God's forgiveness possible. Jesus, the Son of God, gave up His own life so that we might have life and have it more abundantly. When He arose on the third day, the job was completed.

Help me, Lord, to always focus on Your love and forgiveness when painful memories of former events flood my mind. Help me seek Your face and Your word and be reminded of Your promises and Your sacrifice for me.

A Good Name

By Louise Flanders

Bible Reading: Isaiah 45:3-4; Luke 10:20b; Revelation 21:27

"A good name is rather to be chosen than great riches, *and* loving favor rather than silver and gold."

—Proverbs 22:1

For years, my parents related to me the story of my namesake. My family lived in Louisiana when I was born, and my parents became close to their pastor and his family. The couple made a deep impression on my parents, motivating them to name me after the pastor's wife.

My family moved to Texas shortly after my birth, which prevented me from ever knowing my namesake. I thought about her often over the years. Did she remember that I had been named for her? Had she prayed for me to know Christ?

Years later, at the church my husband and I attended, the pastor made an astonishing announcement: "We are honored to have a special retired pastor and his wife visiting with us this evening." My heart felt as though it might explode with joy when I heard their names. At the close of the service, I hurried over to become acquainted with this precious lady I had longed to meet.

I'm thankful to have been named after a woman who devoted her life to ministering alongside her husband. However, I'm even more thankful that Jesus knows my name and it is written in the Lamb's Book of Life. Because I have given my life to Him, I will spend eternity with Him. I am challenged every day to live my life in such a way that I never bring shame to His name or dishonor Him in any way.

Thank You, Father, for knowing my name and knowing me personally. Help me live my life in a way that is pleasing to You.

Tender Hearts

By Dottie Frassetto

Bible Reading: John 11:5-44

"Jesus saith unto her, Said I not unto thee, that, if thou wouldest believe, thou shouldest see the glory of God?"

—John 11:40

It was too late. The funeral was over. Wailing mourners filled the house. Mary and Martha had waited for days, counting on Jesus to heal Lazarus. Disappointment and grief flooded their souls.

When they heard Jesus was coming, Martha ran to meet Him outside the village. She needed answers. You could almost sense an edge to her voice as she said, "Lord, if You had been here, my brother would not have died."

When Martha returned, Mary hurried to meet Jesus. She fell at His feet in tears saying, "Lord, if You had been here, my brother would not have died." Can you sense the difference?

Martha revealed her 'get the job done' heart when she spoke to Jesus, but Mary revealed her tender heart at His feet. Jesus understood both women's hearts. He understands our hearts also.

How do you react when you lose someone or something? Do you strike out in anger, cry inconsolably, or go into denial and handle life as usual? Mary and Martha mourned their brother's death differently; but united in grief, they sought Jesus. Jesus wept with them then raised their brother from the dead. When Lazarus walked out of the tomb, it renewed Mary and Martha's faith in Jesus.

We don't always receive a miracle. God sometimes uses the losses in our lives for His glory. What loss is God using in your life?

Lord, thank You for creating us with different personalities, yet with the same needs. Teach us to respond to each other's needs with the tender heart of Mary, the servant heart of Martha, and the mind of Christ.

Food for the Mind

By Cynthia L. Simmons

Bible Reading: II Timothy 2:1-18

"Study to shew thyself approved unto God, a workman that needeth not to be ashamed, rightly dividing the word of truth."

—II Timothy 2:15

My cat, Mr. Knightly, made a pitiful sound and looked at me with sorrowful eyes.

"Cat! What do you want?" I asked. "I just gave you food—expensive canned cat food."

Mr. Knightly glanced at his dish and gave another sad meow.

"I've had it with you, sir! I've given you the food your doctor prescribed, but you haven't eaten for three days. What am I supposed to do?"

Finally, I changed back to dry food, and Mr. Knightly ate. He didn't get the benefit of the expensive food I had purchased—the food scientists had formulated especially for his needs. He would have been better off with the canned food; but he ate the cheap stuff instead.

Like the specially formulated food the vet prescribed for my cat, the Bible contains food formulated especially for our minds—food we need.

Jesus said, "Man shall not live by bread alone, but by every word that proceedeth out of the mouth of God." In Scripture, God gave us wisdom for each day, hope for eternity, and boundless love. Unfortunately, we don't always feast on God's Word.

The media, like my cat's dry food, can feed our minds, but it can't satisfy our deepest longings. When we study the Bible, the love and grace of God overwhelms our souls. Nothing can satisfy like that. Praise God for His wonderful Word.

Lord, help me grow as I read and study Your Word daily. Thank You for the blessings it contains.

Creator of Heaven and Earth

By Bonnie Greenwood Grant

Bible Reading: Isaiah 45:18; Deuteronomy 31:6

"For thus saith the Lord that created the heavens; God himself that formed the earth and made it; he hath established it, he created it not in vain, he formed it to be inhabited: I *am* the Lord: and *there* is none else."

—Isaiah 45:18

"Be strong and of a good courage, fear not, nor be afraid of them: for the Lord thy God, he *it is* that doth go with thee; he will not fail thee, nor forsake thee."

—Deuteronomy 31:6

I felt depressed. Fear filled my heart…no, more than fear, it was terror that nearly rendered me immobile. *What if there is no God?* I thought. *What if the earth and all its wonders are merely random happenings? What if His voice and all His supposed miracles are just figments of my imagination or examples of hearing and seeing what I wanted to hear and see?* If so, life would lose its joy for me. A heavy pall covered me.

I looked out at the sunlight reflecting off the green leaves and could almost feel the soft breeze that blew them. *How could this just be chemical reactions and molecules bonding randomly?* I wondered.

"Oh, God, please be real," I cried.

The next morning, I opened my e-mails. The first one said, "Bonnie, God told me to send these words (Isaiah 45:18 and Deuteronomy 31:6) to you." God had opened the scriptures to me and had provided me with His answer and His comfort.

Thank You, Lord, for revealing how marvelous Your works—not just Your beautiful earth, but also Your concern for my thoughts and fears—are. You gather me into Your arms so I will not be afraid.

Pillar of Flowers

By Adrienne A. Nelson

Bible Reading: Proverbs 31:10-31

"Strength and honor *are* her clothing; and she shall rejoice in time to come. She openeth her mouth with wisdom; and in her tongue *is* the law of kindness. She looketh well to the ways of her household, and eateth not the bread of idleness. Her children arise up, and call her blessed; her husband *also,* and he praiseth her. Many daughters have done virtuously, but thou excellest them all."

—Proverbs 31:25-29

One Saturday before Mother's Day, my thirteen-year-old son and his friend came into the house and told me they had toured the neighborhood yard sales. It was one of those neighborhood-wide bonanza days for those of us who like to find bargains.

My son said he had helped his friend pick out a Mother's Day gift for his mom, so I said, "Oh, really? What did you get?"

His friend said, "I got her this pillar with flowers on top."

"That sounds nice," I said. Knowing his mother well, I was certain she would find just the right place in her home for that yard sale pillar of flowers. I knew it would remind her of her son's gesture of love and would inspire her to continue being a gentle guide and example for her family—like the kind of mother Proverbs describes.

Beauty is found in correctly building up the mind and the soul and in creating a loving home, as my friend had done. From what other motivation would two thirteen-year-old boys buy a "pillar of flowers?"

Dear Lord, remind me as I pray to lift up all mothers and fathers to You. Please give them strength, wisdom, and Christ-like love.

An Empty Cupboard Filled

By Charlene Elder

Bible Reading: Psalm 34:1-22

"The young lions do lack, and suffer hunger: but they that seek the Lord shall not want any good *thing*."

—Psalm 34:10

My parents didn't have a lot of money when I was growing up, but we never went without food or clothes. They instilled within me a deep trust in God's provision and goodness through their example.

I remember my mom telling me of a particular time when I was very young. There wasn't much food in the house or any milk in the refrigerator. My dad was not due a paycheck for another week. My mom and dad stood in the kitchen and prayed, asking the Lord for His help. They didn't tell anyone else, not even my grandparents.

A couple of hours later, the doorbell rang. To my parent's surprise, the assistant pastor of our church stood on the porch holding a large box filled with food. He shared that the Lord had impressed him to bring us food. At first, he said he was reluctant, but the urging was so strong, he couldn't ignore it. He went to the store, got the food, and brought it to us. There wasn't a dry eye in the house after my parents shared their situation with him. They all stood together in the living room rejoicing and thanking the Lord for His goodness and provision.

My parents continued to trust the Lord for their needs, and He has always provided.

Lord, help me remember to always turn to You first when I have a need, because You are always faithful and will not let me lack any good thing.

You Are Not Alone

By Jack G. Elder

Bible Reading: Psalm 118:4-9

"The Lord is on my side; I will not fear: what can man do unto me?"
—Psalm 118:6

Do you feel like you're all alone facing the cruel world? Do you even feel alone in a crowded room? Often in times of big decisions, you think you're all alone. Maybe you have faced the death of a loved one or the pain of a spouse leaving you. Remember, you are never alone. You have someone on your side to help you face every obstacle in your path.

Isn't it interesting that this verse attacks the fears that come from being alone. The psalmist is a confessor—that is, he states a fact then follows it with a confirming statement. The Lord is on his side, so naturally it creates an overwhelming sense that he has no reason to fear.

Maybe you had to go into a scary place when you were a child, but your dad came with you so you were no longer afraid. That's the way it is with the Lord. You may be facing a scary situation in your life, but the Lord is on your side. You have nothing to fear, not even what man can do to you.

Even if life has totally isolated you, you are not alone. When you face a giant problem, the Lord is on your side. You can confidently say, "No fear for me, thank you."

Thank You, Lord, for being on my side. I will face today's problems knowing that You are with me and care for me. I will not fear.

The Mighty Fortress: A Person

By Marcus Beavers

Bible Reading: Psalm 46

"God is our refuge and strength, a very present help in trouble. Therefore we will not fear…"

—Psalm 46:1-2a

Trouble is rampant in a fallen world; there is always something going wrong. When it does, people are afraid and need help. This psalm is written to show we are to keep trusting the Lord Almighty in all things. Even in tremendous upheavals, we are to trust Him.

When God created the world, He judged it to be very good. But later, certain angels and Adam and Eve caused revolt, sin, and death to enter creation. The good God continues to rule, judge, and redeem His creation. He will lift His voice against the nations, will make wars cease on earth, and will destroy the weapons of war. A time is coming when God will be exalted in the earth.

Martin Luther (1483-1546), the Christian reformer, loved Psalm 46 and turned to it often. He saw God's help amidst many dangers and wrote his wonderful hymn, "A Mighty Fortress is Our God," based on this psalm. The great hymn begins: "A mighty Fortress is our God / a Bulwark never failing/ Our Helper he amid the flood / of mortal ills prevailing."

The infinite, personal God is powerful and loving; His help is real and lasting. He heals broken hearts and gives everlasting life.

Almighty God, Maker of heaven and earth, help me, please, in all my troubles. I want to obey You and do what is right. Take away all fear and give me Your peace.

Better Than an Instant Message

By Pam I. Barnes

Bible Reading: Psalm 55:16-18

"As for me, I will call upon God; and the Lord shall save me."

—Psalm 55:16

Today, our world offers us a full spectrum of communication resources. A few short years ago, only the elite or important individuals had pagers. Cellular or mobile phones were even less common, weighed a ton, or were mounted into our cars. Now everyone—including children—have tiny and versatile cell phones. Most of us have an internet connection at work and/or in our homes that can reach across the globe in seconds.

What does all of this mean? Are we smarter, quicker, better at communicating than people in prior generations? Yes and no. We have the means, but do we have the time it takes to manage it all? E-mail and phone messages pile up quickly, and sending a note in the mail these days seems old-fashioned, not to mention the fact that it now costs 42 cents for a single postage stamp.

Talking to God hasn't changed through the recent technology-booming years. In fact, it hasn't changed through the centuries. He has always been right there. All we've ever needed to do was trust Him and have faith, pray, and believe. Connecting with God is better than sending Instant Messages! We simply need to turn down our radios, televisions, and I-pods, and move away from our computers, and make time to talk to Him.

Dear God, I am thankful to know You hear my prayers. Thank You for the world I live in. Please help me as I face constant challenges in difficult times. I need Your guidance in all that I do. Please bless my health, my future, and my life. In Jesus' name I pray.

Daily Renewal

By Brenda Thompson Ward

Bible Reading: II Corinthians 4:7-18

"For which cause we faint not; but though our outward man perish, yet the inward *man* is renewed day by day."

—II Corinthians 4:16

This verse gives a wonderful assurance to the believer during times of trouble. I needed that verse for a number of days because of all the pollen floating around. My "outward man" couldn't breathe without a humidifier and nasal spray. My eyes watered and itched, and my voice was much deeper than usual. The verse encouraged me, because I knew that even if my natural body fought with nature, my spiritual self, my "inward man," could be renewed.

One of the most comforting aspects of being a Christian to me is living each day with "eternity values" in view. My sufferings are pale in comparison to the heavenly joys God has stored up for me.

Our lives will take on a new meaning when we see things through God's eyes. Christians are the only people who can be renewed on a daily basis. We can accept the fact that we are growing older each day and that someday we will die; but the joy is that heaven awaits us. With this in mind—even when we awake feeling as though we've been whipped with a heavy stick—we can praise God for the reality that our "inward man" can draw strength daily from God's Word and the Holy Spirit.

Lord, help me not get so involved with the problems and "afflictions" of daily life that I forget about the strength I can draw from You. Please help me remember that my soul can be renewed daily.

My He-man

By Robert W. Ellis

Bible Reading: Hebrews 13:5

"…for he hath said, I will never leave thee, nor forsake thee."

—Hebrews 13:5b

Genealogy is important to the Jewish people and to God, so you will be faced with many names as you read through the Bible. Most of the names will not be recognizable, and many of them may elicit a smile. Two of my favorites from the Old Testament are Buzi and Bunni.

I ran across another name recently that caused me to stop, smile, and reflect. The name was Heman. He-man was a term I heard during my youth. It meant a man equal to John Wayne and other western heroes. He-man is not used today. I suppose it is not politically correct. Heman in the Bible had fourteen sons and three daughters. You might think…*hence the name Heman.*

Having lots of children does not make you a He-man, as we know. *My* favorite earthly he-man had only one son…me. You see, my father was a true he-man, at least in my eyes.

As my wife and I struggled through early marriage days with three babies less than eighteen months old, Dad was there to help us carry the load. He washed and dried clothes, took babies to the doctor, and helped with bills on occasion. He was a real he-man.

My favorite he-man passed away at a young age and left us with only memories of his courageous acts. Jesus promised to never leave us alone to fend for ourselves. We can trust that to be the case. He will be our he-man to the very end.

Thank You, Lord, for being my trusted friend, my he-man, my hero, and my Savior.

New Beginnings

By Patty Rocco

Bible Reading: II Corinthians 5; Lamentations 3

"Therefore if any man be in Christ, he is a new creature: old things are passed away; behold, all things are become new."

—II Corinthians 5:17

New trainees filed into the room, taking their seats at tables set up in the shape of a horseshoe. Freshly sharpened pencils lay across brand new tablets for note taking. Never-used service manuals and handbooks lay underneath the tablets with fresh-from-the-box highlighters and pens.

Many of the trainees were newly retired, nervously embarking on a new chapter of life. Yet, each one brought with them an excitement of regeneration that electrified the air. As introductions were made around the table, it became evident that we all needed another chance.

That is why Jesus came into the world—to give mankind a second chance to relate to the Father. God continues to extend new beginnings, even when we have wrinkles. His mercies are new every morning. Even those of us at an older age can become as excited as young school children, because the character of God overflows with mercy.

Father, thank You for extending great mercies to me every morning. Thank You that in Christ I am a new creature: old things have passed away. You continue to make me new. I bless Your Name because You are the God of second chances.

Building Bigger Barns

By Burl McCosh

Bible Reading: Luke 12:15-21

"And he (a certain rich man) thought within himself, saying, What shall I do, because I have no room where to bestow my fruits? And he said, This will I do: I will pull down my barns, and build greater; and there will I bestow all my fruits and my goods'."

—Luke 12:17-18

A few years ago, I began to accumulate things. I bought many assorted tools, and I stored up scrap building supplies that I had salvaged. I thought I was becoming well prepared to accomplish future personal projects.

I eventually had to look beyond the house boundaries to store the accumulated items, so I contracted for a barn to be built on my property. Upon its completion, I proceeded to move things into it. Of course, this gave me additional space to accumulate more project paraphernalia.

Jesus tells us in Luke 12:15, "Take heed, and beware of covetousness: for a man's life consisteth not in the abundance of the things which he possesseth." That was a lesson that I was to learn the hard way. During that time, I had a life experience that made all of the accumulated stuff seem worthless. It actually became a burden, and all I wanted to do was dispose of it.

In the parable in Luke, the rich man could not use his treasure, and he could not take it with him. Real treasure does not lie in the things of this world. Real treasure is what we posses in Christ.

Dear Lord, remind me daily that it is not the things of this world that are important. Help me not strive to lay up personal treasure, but to use Your provision to glorify You.

The Hand of God

By Judy Becker

*Bible Reading: Exodus 8:16-19; Exodus 31:18;
Deuteronomy 9:10; Psalm 8:3-4; Luke 11:20*

"Thy right hand, O Lord, is become glorious in power: thy right hand, O Lord, hath dashed in pieces the enemy."

—Exodus 15:6

We sing the song, "Who is like unto Thee, O Lord, among the gods?...glorious in holiness… doing wonders?" This verse follows the verse in our scripture focus and the next verse speaks of His stretched out hand causing the earth to swallow enemies. Clearly, God's power rests in His hand.

If you look up "a mighty hand and stretched out arm" in a concordance, you will find multiple references to the word picture of the "hand" referring to the Holy Spirit and the "arm" referring to Jesus. In Isaiah 53:1-5 we read, "To whom is the arm of the Lord revealed, for he…a man of sorrows…was wounded for our transgressions." Working together and showing mighty wonders of power, the "hand" and "arm" brought the children of Israel out of Egypt.

The prophets said, "the hand of the Lord was upon me," meaning the *power* of the Holy Spirit was upon them. Jesus said to the Pharisees, "If I, with the finger of God, cast out demons, no doubt the kingdom of God is come upon you."

There are four mentions of the fingers of God in today's scripture reading. God created life, like the lice in Egypt; He created the heavens with His fingers; He wrote the Ten Commandments with His own finger; He exercises all authority over principalities with His finger. God's hand is indeed mighty.

Father, help me remember that Your hand is powerful enough to do all things.

How Much Do You Weigh?

By Margaret Fagre

Bible Reading: John 12:32

"A stone is heavy, and the sand weighty; but a fool's wrath is heavier than them both."

—Proverbs 27:3

When I asked, "How much do you weigh," I did not mean body weight. It is good to be physically healthy; however, I am talking about how much your spirit weighs.

In Proverbs, we read that a fool's wrath is heavier than sand and stone. I do not know how much a fool's wrath weighs, but I do know that when my heart is full of anger or fear, I feel like I am carrying a heavy load. There is a general feeling of heaviness and pain.

I do not want to be like Haman, the villain in the story of Queen Esther. In Esther 3:5, it is recorded that Haman was full of wrath. I know that Haman's spirit was very heavy. I am very grateful that the Lord has provided a weight loss program. Whenever I repent and turn back towards the Lord, my spirit feels lighter and lighter.

I swim three times a week to stay physically fit. I pray, study the scriptures, and serve my family, friends, and neighbors to keep my spirit light, agile, and in shape.

In Ephesians 4:19, we read that some were past feeling. I don't want to reach the point where I would not want to take advantage of the Lord's weight loss program and repent. When I repent, I know the Lord will take my burden and lift me up.

I am grateful to You, Lord, that You were lifted up on the cross. I am grateful that You draw all men unto Yourself. Thank You for the principle of repentance.

BEAR ONE ANOTHER'S BURDENS

By Louise Flanders

Bible Reading: James 5:14-16; Matthew 25:35-45

"Bear ye one another's burdens, and so fulfill the law of Christ."
—Galatians 6:2

One by one the people came until the room overflowed and more chairs had to be added. We had all arrived with one purpose. A precious friend had been diagnosed with lung cancer, and we had gathered at her home to pray for her and offer words of encouragement.

Several in the group had experienced the devastating effects of cancer first-hand, and their testimonies were powerful. Mike, who had undergone a radiation treatment that very morning, related that he praised God for his cancer because of the lessons God had taught him through the experience. Ralph shared that nothing else in his life had ever brought him closer to God. Both testified that lessons learned during the darkest times of their lives had matured their faith and strengthened their relationship with God.

Others shared of God's faithfulness in their lives. Then we took turns praying for our friend. We asked God to fill her with His peace, to grant a miracle of healing, and to give each of us a deeper relationship with the One who created us.

God's Word instructs us to "bear one another's burdens" and to pray for those who are sick. As we joined hands and sang a hymn, we knew that God had been honored, and we had been blessed as we had prayed for our friend.

Father, help me have a heart that is sensitive to the needs of those around me. Help me be willing to set aside time to pray for those who are sick and for those who are bearing heavy burdens.

Proving Our Love

By Susan M. Schulz

Bible Reading: John 14:15-21

"If you love me, keep my commandments."

—John 14:15

"Ruby, come," I called.

My border collie perked her ears and came running. The moment she noticed the treat in my hand, she repeatedly leapt into midair. If Ruby could talk, she would say, "Hurry up, tell me what to do. I love you and want to please you."

Ruby went on to her other trick of grabbing her tail and spinning in circles at lightening speed. I gave her another command, "Ruby, jump and spin." After Ruby leapt and turned in midair, I delivered the tidbit, which she gobbled down.

Ruby loves us as much as we love her, maybe more. Thinking about her love brought the truth that is planted throughout the New Testament to my mind. Jesus tells us that if we love Him, we will obey Him.

Why does the word *obey* conjure up a negative picture of a master and his dog? I often balk at being told what to do and when to do it. But as the verse above shows, love is proven by obedience.

God gives us the power to obey, even on those days when we feel like an old dog that can't learn anything new. We are *never* too old or set in our ways to learn the depth of Jesus' love.

Jesus, I praise You for being my perfect example. You loved Your Father so much You obeyed Him, even to Your death on a cruel cross. Give me strength to obey Your commands each day. I desire to prove my love to You.

A New Song to Sing

By Charlene Elder

Bible Reading: Psalm 96:1-13

"O sing unto the Lord a new song: sing to the Lord, all the earth. Sing unto the Lord, bless his name; shew forth his salvation from day to day. Declare his glory among the heathen, his wonders among all people."

—Psalm 96:1-3

I've always loved to sing, but I now recognize that my voice and range aren't what they used to be. I definitely wouldn't make it in a talent contest. Nowadays, I make a joyful—but less than perfect—noise unto the Lord when I sing; but I still sing.

Whether your voice is fantastic or mediocre, you can sing a new song unto the Lord and proclaim His name among the people. When you praise the Lord in song or just in words without music, you exalt Him above the problems you face, the situations you're in, and the difficulties you endure.

David didn't suggest that we sing a new song of praise to the Lord. He commanded us to DO IT. Three amazing things happen when you praise the Lord—it exalts the Lord, it lifts you up, and it keeps the enemy at bay.

When you face a tough day or hard times, sing a new song and praise the Lord. You'll discover an exhilarating freedom as you praise Him!

With my voice, Lord, I will exalt You, giving the praise of my lips for all that You have done for me. You are worthy to be praised. Each day I will praise You.

Relationship With God

By Mildred McDonald-Carter

Bible Reading: Ephesians 2:12-14

"That at that time ye were without Christ, being aliens from the commonwealth of Israel, and strangers from the covenants of promise, having no hope, and without God in the world: But now in Christ Jesus ye who sometimes were far off are made nigh by the blood of Christ."

—Ephesians 2:12-14

The death of a loved one has a different effect on different individuals. After my mother's death, I felt lonely and had a "don't care" attitude. Eventually, I began to work more and failed to do my daily Bible reading. Then the Holy Spirit convinced me to resume my daily reading of the New Testament.

When I read Matthew 11:28-30, the Holy Spirit said, "Write that down," and I did. From that October until December, the Holy Spirit directed me to write down specific scriptures. In December, I wanted to create calendars, and the Holy Spirit reminded me of those scriptures. I was able to produce 12 titled poems. Through them the Lord was telling me a story.

He said to come to Him and my burdens would be light; and that being against the Holy Spirit was not forgiven. He reminded me that I must believe to receive and that love is the greatest commandment. He told me that I must be saved and reminded me how blessed I was. I was shown what my priorities should be and told how I should deal with others. He showed me what type person I am when I come to the Word, and He reminded me that He did say to "ask." Finally, I was told how the Kingdom could be destroyed.

Father, Your loving kindness and guidance helped me through a difficult period. Thank You. Through Jesus Christ, I am at now peace.

A New Creature

By Judy Parrott

Bible Reading: II Corinthians 5

"Therefore if any man *be* in Christ, *he* is a new creature: old things are passed away; behold, all things are become new."

—II Corinthians 5:17

I taught third grade Sunday school for a year before it came to the pastor's attention that some teachers were not born again. I was often asked if I was a Christian, and my standard answer was, "Of course I am a blankety-blank Christian." I was insulted that they could possibly think I was a heathen. After all, I was raised in the church. If anyone asked me who Jesus was, my answer was, "How in the ____ do I know?"

Then the teachers were required to attend a week of evening meetings, structured for some of us to accept Christ without public embarrassment. By the end of the week, I realized something essential was missing in my life. On Sunday morning, the pastor preached this salvation message: "Every man has been given a measure of faith. Shut your eyes and imagine reaching your hand up to heaven and having Jesus grab it." I did that, and suddenly I knew that Jesus had taken my hand. It was a profound spiritual experience that introduced me to Jesus at the age of thirty-two.

It took six months after that for me to completely stop cursing, but every time I swore, I wept and repented. I finally realized I was grieving the Holy Spirit. He changed my heart and my mouth began to speak His words.

Dear Lord, I am grateful that You are in charge of changing me, and all I need to do is cooperate with You. Thank You for the gift of faith, for my wonderful life, and for hope for eternity.

My Joyful Noise

By Darlene Applegate

Bible Reading: Psalm 98:1-9

"Make a joyful noise unto the Lord, all the earth: make a loud noise, and rejoice, and sing praise. Sing unto the Lord with the harp, and the voice of a psalm. With trumpets and sound of cornet make a joyful noise before the Lord, the King."

—Psalm 98:4-6

My heart was filled with thanksgiving to the Lord, as it was most Sundays; but something was different that day. As I belted out songs of praise, I opened my eyes and saw that my singing had embarrassed my family. After that, I sang quietly under my breath, not wanting to annoy anyone else.

Later, in my prayer time, the Lord took me to Psalms. When I read the verses above, I knew I had offended the Lord by not giving Him my highest praise and worship. I shared with my family what God had shown me and told them I hoped they wouldn't be offended, but from that time on I was going to praise God with my best voice. Even though I still sang off key, my family members smiled when I sang because they understood that I loved the Lord and was giving Him my best.

Since that time, I make no apology for my voice. It is the voice God gave me, and He loves to hear me sing, talk, and praise Him with all that I am. After all, the scripture says, "make a joyful noise." That is what I do.

Father, lift up those who stop short when singing praises to Your name. Break them out of the bondage of fear so they may worship You with all they are.

Equal Spoils

By Susan M. Watkins

Bible Reading: I Samuel 30:21-25

"For who will harken unto you in this matter? but as his part *is* that goeth down to the battle, so *shall* his part *be* that tarrieth by the stuff: they shall part alike."

—I Samuel 30:24

God masterfully levels the playing field and reigns Supreme over His creation. He is ever focused on equality in His handiwork. He did not give Adam dominion over Eve. He made them joint-rulers. This same theme was woven into the fabric of David's heart as he dealt with his army. Urged by other voices to elevate the warrior's share above those stationed to oversee the army's supplies, David silenced their segregation. They would all share equally, rewarded with equal risk taken. Fresh memories of his pasture days—caring for sheep and singing praises to God—bathed his kingly decisions. He had not forgotten, nor had his heart hardened or turned.

This concept is important to God. It is only heard by wise ears. Ears tuned to giving and not to self-promotion. Ears with power to abuse that choose not to. Those who understand the necessity of structural support within a sound building know that without reliable ribs upon which to stand, the burden of the weight would cause the entire edifice to collapse. God's plumb line is precise. His toolbox—literally out of this world. We are His palace; His dwelling place. All are equal in His presence.

If you've struggled and questioned your importance, know that King David, described by God as chasing after His own heart, recognizes and supports you. Also know that The King knows exactly who you are and that you are qualified to do exactly what you're doing. There's no one else equipped to do what you alone can do!

Father, help me see Your capable reflection when I view myself.

Problem Solver

By Toni Kiriakopoulos

Bible Reading: I Thessalonians 5:17; Deuteronomy 11:27; John 15:12

"But seek ye first the kingdom of God, and his righteousness; and all these things shall be added unto you."

—Matthew 6:33

How often do we seek God's Kingdom? It is really very simple to do. We must simply follow God's rules: put God first, obey the commandments, love one another, and pray without ceasing.

When we do not seek God, we cannot find Him; yet God is always there. Often we get caught up in our busy lives and don't take enough time to go to the problem solver. He is the answer to every need.

Christ left us with the glorious gift of prayer. We know that when we pray, things happen. We may not always get the answers we want, but we will get God's answers. We may pray for something with which God does not agree. At those times we must trust Him and His answers because He knows best.

When we walk with God and we obey, He adds to our lives peace, joy, and the ability to victoriously walk through trials. The problem solver is always waiting to spend time with us.

Lord, help me seek the things of the Kingdom. Put a hunger in my heart for Your Word. Help me pray without ceasing. Help me be a servant of Jesus.

The Hiding Place

By Brenda Thompson Ward

Bible Reading: Psalm 32

"Thou *art* my hiding place; Thou *shalt* preserve me from trouble; thou shalt compass me about with songs of deliverance. Selah."

—Psalm 32:7

In January of 2000, I was told I had a malignant melanoma on my left retina. I will never forget the closed-in feeling I experienced. I could hear my husband and the doctor talking about treatment, but my reaction was, "Lord, I'm going to die." Then that still, small voice inside whispered and said, "Brenda, if you died, would that be so bad?"

I left the doctor's office in tears. I was frightened beyond description. I knew how it felt to be backed into a corner without an escape route. I knew the doctors were great in their field; still, I needed something they couldn't give.

The next morning, I was thrilled and amazed when I came upon Psalm 32. That was exactly what I needed. Doctors are great, and the fact that I had a treatable cancer was encouraging; however, I needed the Great Physician. That morning I found peace in knowing that I had a hiding place—a place to let go of my fear and get to the point of saying, "Okay Lord, whatever you want is all right with me. I know the doctors can do their part, but You can do even greater things."

During that time, I learned that regardless of what happens in my life, God is always there waiting for me to turn to Him. He is my strength and my hiding place. God has since blessed me with six cancer-free years.

Lord, thank You for the peace and comfort I draw from You in trying times. Let me never forget Your love and concern for me. Help me remember to draw my strength from You.

The Joy of Giving

By Diana J. Baker

Bible Reading: Psalm 118:5; Genesis 12:2; Mark 12:41-44

"Give and it shall be given unto you; good measure, pressed down, and shaken together, and running over, shall men give into your bosom. For with the same measure that ye mete withal it shall be measured to you again."

—Luke 6:38

I have noticed that doing something nice for someone else lifts my spirits. It's difficult to dwell on my problems and needs when I reach beyond myself to meet the needs of others.

Years ago, one of my minister friends sank into a deep depression. His nights became nightmares, as sleep evaded him and unsettling thoughts raced through his mind. He struggled through weary days, trying to stay awake and functional after those sleepless nights.

Late one evening, he stood staring out the window at a street light and God spoke to him. God told my friend that if he wanted to be set free from depression, he needed to go "across the tracks" and find someone in worse shape than he was in and help that person. My friend's obedience to that command set him free.

I often become caught up in my own circumstances and needs and forget that God called me not only to be blessed but also to be a blessing. If I desire to live a life of blessing and wholeness, I must plant good seeds in other people's lives. As I plant those seeds, God will multiply them to bring an abundant harvest in my life and in the lives of others.

Dear Father, thank You for the abundant blessings You have poured into my life through Your Son, Jesus Christ. Please help me give to others as abundantly as You have given to me.

Really Giving

By Patty Rocco

Bible Reading: Matthew 6:1-4

"But when thou doest alms, let not thy left hand know what thy right hand doeth: That thine alms may be in secret: and thy Father which seeth in secret himself shall reward thee openly."

—Matthew 6:3-4

When we think about giving, we often think of money, but there is so much more to giving than that. We met Jerome through his daughter, Geraldine, after she and I had become close friends. He and his wife invited our family for Thanksgiving dinner.

We were invited to move to Georgia some years later by my dad, with whom we struggled to maintain a relationship. Closing in the miles didn't seem to help. God's answer to that prayer seemed slow, but I realized later that it was right on time.

Whenever I visited Geraldine, we would head north to see Jerome. He called me his "Georgia Peach." Without words, Jerome taught me to look at tough relationships from different angles. I learned to enjoy Jerome as a father figure. Since there were no expectations, all I needed to do was enjoy the interaction. It was as if God set me in a classroom to learn about earthly fathers and to learn to love unconditionally like my Heavenly Father does. My dad and I now talk almost every day.

Many think God is scrutinizing our lives, when He is simply asking us to enjoy the interaction with Him. When we look at Him from the different angles of His Word, we become more appreciative of who He is. He becomes the Father we want to know better.

Thank You, Father, for using others to help my relationship with You grow. Thank You, Lord, for healing my hurts through the classroom of life.

Ravens on Assignment

By Susan M. Watkins

Bible Reading: I Kings 17:2-6

"And it shall be, *that* thou shalt drink of the brook; and I have commanded the ravens to feed thee there."

—I Kings 17:4

Are you encountering problems with the "doves" in your life? Do you find they're not feeding you according to your needs, but are actually contributing to your problems? God understands. He also knows our reluctance to receive from unexpected sources. It's easy to disregard an unfamiliar fountainhead thinking it doesn't have His authorship. We apply the brakes and rationalize; but God still sends ravens on assignment.

The Lord removed Elijah from his enemies and hid him in the wilderness beside a brook. He had a water source; but since he wasn't called to fast, he needed groceries. His obedience kept him stationed and his sustenance was provided from an unforeseen origin. In the midst of famine, meat was on his menu—meat for a man shielded by God, while his enemy sought his life.

The only table affording meat was the king's. God orchestrated ravens to apprehend the monarch's wealth and beak-deliver it to his sworn enemy—every single day! It's impossible to suppress a smile when we discover the tinkerings of God from His elaborate, celestial throne room.

Had Elijah objected, he'd have starved. God's provisions are creative—bringing water from Moses' rock was just the beginning. We're free to accept or reject the vessel through which God blesses us. It's not only the doves that pour into our lives, but often the ravens. To limit God's designation stunts our blessing. He longs to show us mercy, and we must be receptive to whatever frequency He uses to transmit it.

Lord, thank You. Your ways exceed my vision, and Your love for me never recedes.

Fearfully and Wonderfully Made

By Jack G. Elder

Bible Reading: Psalm 139:11-16

"I will praise thee; for I am fearfully *and* wonderfully made: marvelous are thy works; and *that* my soul knoweth right well."

—Psalm 139:14

The adult body is made up of an estimated 100 trillion cells, which are constantly dying and reforming. The same body has 600 muscles and 206 bones. There are approximately 100,000 miles of arteries and a pump, which propels 300 quarts of blood an hour through the system and will beat some 2,700,000,000 beats in a lifetime. There are lymph systems, nerve systems, optical systems, complicated organs, and much more in the intricately designed body.

God created our wonderful bodies, adapted to their environment. One would have to take an impossible leap of faith to believe that all this came by chance or by evolution.

When David, the King of Israel, wrote this Psalm, he praised God for what he perceived was a marvelous work of God. David fearfully or reverently attributed this creation to the wonderful imagination and design of the creator of all things.

Every day we should give praise to God for our health and life and take nothing for granted, as we are the wondrous works of God. It is a marvelous fact. Just think of what our heavenly Father had in mind when He made us. That is certainly a cause for praise.

Father, thank You for all the complicated parts of my body, which were designed by You for my health and happiness. Help me never forget the source of my life. I praise You for every beat of my heart.

A Tree Falls in the Forest

By Pam I. Barnes

Bible Reading: Matthew 22:37-39

"Jesus said unto him, Thou shalt love the Lord thy God with all thy heart, and with all thy soul, and with all thy mind."

—Matthew 22:37

Scientific theory or proven fact? Believe it or disagree? Can you prove it, disprove it, or do you simply have a feeling about it?

We are so ready to have an opinion these days. Any topic can become material for debate. Whether reading about movie stars, sports figures, or anyone in the news, we are used to forming opinions on the headline topics.

I remember in school many years ago when we studied principles of sound. The teacher asked, "If a tree in the forest fell and no one was there to hear it, would it make a sound?" That was mind-boggling to our seventh grade class. We couldn't prove silence or sound, because we would have had to have been in the forest in order to know if there was sound or not; yet if we had been there, it would have made proving the theory impossible.

God is always with us, and He listens to us. If we create space for open communication and prepare our hearts to listen to Him, we'll "hear" His Word and feel His nudging, His encouragement, and His love. We don't have to prove anything to know He is there.

God's actions and reactions in our lives should be all the witness we need in order to know we are His, and He is our faithful protector, our adviser, our Lord, and our Master.

Dear Lord, please accept my thanks for Your abiding presence. I pray for Your will to be done in my life as I walk with You, love You, and serve You.

Spiritual Battle

By Cynthia L. Simmons

Bible Reading: Ephesians 6:1–9

"For we wrestle not against flesh and blood, but against principalities, against powers, against rulers of the darkness of this world..."

—Ephesians 6:12

Dark, frightening images filled my mind, and I couldn't think. I had planned to pray, but I stopped. Fear tingled up and down my spine and words wouldn't come. I had intended to start painting my bathroom later in the day, but I needed to remove a large mirror on the wall first, because the backing was coming off. The builder had glued the mirror to the wall, and I'd wondered how easily it would come down. Just as I had started to pray, horrid pictures had flashed into my mind. I saw the mirror coming off the wall in huge broken slices, leaving gaping holes in the wall.

"Lord, I don't think these fearful thoughts are from You. Please, help me pray. I need to take down the mirror today. Please, help me do that without problems. But right now, please help me pray!"

As soon as I prayed those words, the ghastly images vanished and the cold fear disappeared. I had my usual prayer time and about an hour later, my son helped me take down the mirror. It came down without breaking or damaging the sheetrock. I believe Satan had tried to prevent my prayer time by sending horrid images to terrify me. God took the fear and discomfort the moment I cried out to Him. He heard my desperate cry.

"Lord, help me pray even when it's hard. Remind me about the spiritual battle that surrounds me. Protect me from Satan's power."

Jesus Knows My Name

By Margaret Fagre

Bible Reading: John 10:27

"Furthermore we have had fathers of our flesh which corrected *us*, and we gave *them* reverence: shall we not much rather be in subjection unto the Father of spirits, and live?"

—Hebrews 12:9

Margaret Louise Alexander Fagre—whose name is that? You may not know that name, but the Lord knows my name. How is that possible? Father in Heaven is all knowing, and He is the Father of my spirit. He knows my name and your name also.

When a politician is running for office and wants me to vote for him, he has to convince me that he knows me and will represent me. He may shake my hand at a rally or even knock on my door, but when he takes a stand on issues that are important to me, I feel like he knows me and cares about what I care about.

When the Lord gives me answers to my prayers, I feel like He is knocking on my door. When the Lord blesses me with what I need most of all, then I know that He knows who I am, because He gives me exactly what I need.

When I am convinced that the Lord knows who I am and cares about me, then I am motivated to follow Him. He is my Father, and I am his daughter. We speak the same language, and I can hear His voice.

Please help me be still and quiet so I can hear Your voice. Help me know that whatever happens in my life, You know me, and I matter to You. Please help me follow You.

Hearing Moses and the Prophets

By Marcus Beavers

Bible Reading: Luke 16:19-31

"Abraham saith unto him, They have Moses and the prophets; let them hear them."

—Luke 16:29

For many years, I could not hear Moses and the prophets. I attended a great number of church services, but never understood. It took personal problems, a Christian community, and one who proclaimed the gospel in a clear way to enable me to pause and listen, then to bow, repent, and believe.

Jesus—God the Son—spoke with authority about hell, a place of torment. He told a parable about a rich man who had enjoyed good things on earth, but had given no heed to Moses and the prophets—representatives of the one true God of Abraham. In life, the rich man had evidently known about the beggar, Lazarus, at his gate, but had shown him no compassion. Preoccupied with earthly things, he had disregarded ultimate things.

In hell after his death, the rich man saw Lazarus being comforted in Paradise beside Abraham. He worried about his living kin and asked Abraham to send someone to warn them. Abraham said if they wouldn't hear Moses and the prophets, they wouldn't even believe one raised from the dead.

In Abraham's final answer, Christ poignantly emphasized how many would not believe when He was raised from the dead on the third day. They would be deaf and blind to Moses and the prophets and would live as though their present, fallen existence were the only final reality.

God in Heaven, thank You for sending Christ, the Eternal Son, to die for my sins. I want to understand Your truth in the Bible and obey You. Help me to love mercy and justice and to care for others as You have commanded.

Missing Keys — Lost or Misplaced?

By Pam I. Barnes

Bible Reading: Jeremiah 29:11-14

"And ye shall seek me, and find *me*, when ye shall search for me with all your heart."

—Jeremiah 29:13

I could not believe my keys were lost again. Where could they be? This act of frantic searching was becoming common, and it seemed to happen when I seriously needed to be on my way.

Surely someone must have stolen them, or they would be hanging by the garage door or safely tucked away in my briefcase. If someone *had* taken them, I wouldn't be guilty of being careless with something so important—again. But if that were true, worse problems could potentially develop regarding the security of my home and property.

Tracing my steps several times, I found nothing. I was becoming impatient, stressed, and worried. I knew if I prayed for God's help, took a deep breath, and looked once more, I would find the missing keys.

Sure enough, there they were, right underneath the huge stack of mail I had literally dropped on the kitchen table. I breathed in relief and rushed out the door. As I cranked the car, I took a moment to say a prayer of thanks. I felt God's peace.

Dear Heavenly Father, please forgive me for the times I "misplace" or "lose" my faith in You as I lost my keys. I know You are there for me, if only I slow down and hear Your voice. Please help me make time for prayer and faith and keep me from letting other things pile up or get in the way. You are my "keys" to all things that matter in life. I love You, Lord.

Sequestered in Silence

By Susan M. Watkins

Bible Reading: Exodus 2:1-10

"And the woman conceived, and bare a son: and when she saw him that he was a goodly child, she hid him three months."

—Exodus 2:2

God's apron contains a secret pocket which serves a most unusual purpose. It's where He hides us for a season. He tenderly slips us out of view, concealing our whereabouts while He orchestrates our destiny. Moses was hidden during his life—three months as an infant; forty years on the backside of the desert. All was divinely on course.

At times, we need to be obscured from enemies. In God's hidden chamber we grow deeply, becoming strong. Often, we misinterpret the time as a dead or inactive season. In reality, it is a time of loving protection fueled by profuse growth. It's also a time of ethereal silence. Questions remain unanswered, and we impatient sheep call God's character into question. He alone understands what must transpire for our success. He keeps His merciful eye on the triumphant goal.

The testing of our faith is the greatest gift God bestows. It alone can produce endurance. The seasoned athlete knows the laurel wreath is awarded solely to the unrelenting winner who has endured to the end. It's an exacting education with monumental results. The purpose is refinement.

Moses emerged from his hidden season with a character of steel, which was necessary to free and lead millions to prepared liberty. During his training, God met his needs for marriage and fatherhood.

If you're wrestling with deafening silence, allow yourself to be hidden by God. His single focus is your maturation, and His well-established history sings of His stable faithfulness. Willingly slide into His secret pocket for His glory.

Father, teach me to trust the stillness of Your undertakings.

Pictures of Love

By Louise Flanders

Bible Reading: I Corinthians 13:1-13; Ephesians 5:25-33; I Peter 3:7

"Husbands, love your wives, even as Christ also loved the church, and gave himself for it."

—Ephesians 5:25

I can still see them sitting at the kitchen table, Mother with one hand extended, fingers spread wide apart, and Daddy carefully applying bright red polish to each nail.

Mother had received a diagnosis of diabetes too late to stop the damage to her eyes. In spite of multiple laser treatments, she eventually became legally blind. Daddy, though not a patient person by nature, not only treated her to a manicure each week, but he also carefully applied her make-up each morning before they left the house. He frequently applied rouge and lipstick a little too generously, but the end result was not as important as the act of love it represented.

My husband, Johnny, and I have been married over forty years. In all those years, he has never forgotten to celebrate an important date in October. It's not our wedding anniversary or either of our birthdays. The special date he always remembers with a card or dinner out is the anniversary of the date he proposed.

God not only instructed husbands to love their wives and honor them, but in I Peter 3:7, He promised a reward to those who obeyed the commandment. He promised those obedient husbands that their prayers would not be hindered. This kind of love between a husband and wife paints a beautiful picture for the world of Christ's love for His bride, the Church.

Thank You, Father, for the supreme example of love that You gave to us by sending Your Son to pay the price for our sins.

Angels Among Us

By Judy Parrott

Bible Reading: Psalm 34:1-10; Hebrews 1:14

"The angel of the Lord encampeth around about them that fear him, and delivereth them."

—Psalm 34:7

Are angels real? Many Christians claim to have seen angels or to have had experiences involving angels.

A man in our motorcycle group broadsided a pickup truck that ran a stop sign and flew across his path at about 60 miles per hour. Pete's motorcycle was demolished, but Pete was transported miraculously over the truck and landed on his feet without a scratch on the other side of the truck.

A policeman came to the scene and asked, "Where is the victim?"

Pete answered, "Here I am."

"No, I mean the dead guy that was on the cycle," the policeman said.

"It's me!" Pete said.

Was that an angel encounter? Psalm 91:11 says, "For he shall give his angels charge over thee, to keep thee in all thy ways."

Another incident happened while my husband was standing outside his hotel in New York City. A man was lying under a parked Mercedes helping the owner tie up a fallen muffler when the jack unexpectedly collapsed, and he was trapped beneath the car. Two men tried to lift the four-thousand-pound car, but couldn't budge it. Suddenly, a man drove up on a motor scooter, parked, ran to the Mercedes and lifted it high enough for the men to pull the victim out. Some say an adrenalin rush can produce supernatural strength, but the real fact is that God's angels are continually working on our behalf. I believe the man who lifted the car was an angel or was assisted by an angel.

Dear Lord, thank You for sending Your angels to protect us. Help us remember we are never alone.

Confident Prayer

By Charlene Elder

Bible Reading: John 15:1-7

"If ye abide in me, and my words abide in you, ye shall ask what ye will, and it shall be done unto you."

—John 15:7

Have you ever realized how practical and concerned God is with the everyday events in our lives?

One Saturday morning, I was at my daughter's home babysitting my grandchildren while my daughter went to pick up her daughter, Aleena, at preschool. Their doggie, JoJo, joined me on the couch as I fed the youngest.

Later, we heard the garage door open as they returned, and we all headed to the garage to greet them. Once inside the house, we couldn't find JoJo. She didn't come when we called her name.

We searched inside and outside. She was nowhere to be found. *Oh, Lord, please take care of JoJo* I silently prayed. *You know where she is. Please bring her home safely. Don't let her get hurt. This family needs their JoJo!*

My heart was broken because I thought I had let her slip out of the house and garage and hadn't noticed. *Lord, please bring JoJo back.* My daughter had gone up the street but didn't see her. When she went out a second time, I prayed again. *Lord, please let my daughter find her. You know where JoJo is—keep her safe.* When my daughter returned, I broke into tears of thanksgiving as I saw JoJo run into the house. She was back home—safe and sound.

Lord, I will pray when I have a need and trust that You will answer me. Thank You because You are concerned with every aspect of my life.

Assurance of Tomorrow

By Brenda Thompson Ward

Bible Reading: Proverbs 27:1; James 4:13-17

"Boast not thyself of tomorrow; for thou knowest not what a day may bring forth."

—Proverbs 27:1

Years ago, I heard an evangelist say that we should live every day as though we could be taken out of this life at any second. Facing cancer helped instill that attitude into my life.

We all make plans and prepare for the future. However, we should never leave God out of our plans.

It would be foolish not to plan for the future. We need savings plans for buying or renovating a home, for investments, for retirement funds, etc. And because we love our families, we have health insurance, life insurance, and home insurance.

However, we don't always make plans to invest in the spiritual lives of those we love. It's wonderful to prepare for the unexpected things of life, but we should never neglect to talk to our loved ones about their relationship with the Lord.

I'm glad I talked to my brother before he died. My heart was broken when we were told he had only a few weeks to live. Usually, it's not difficult for me to express myself, but I was nervous about broaching the subject of salvation with my brother, although I desperately needed to know if he was a Christian and if I'd see him again in eternity.

I spoke to him and found out that he was a born again Christian and knew where he would spend eternity. It would have been a shame if I had not talked to my brother. Now I know I will see him in heaven.

Thank you, Lord, for extending my life. Help me live it with the knowledge that every minute is a precious gift.

Talk to Me

By Robert W. Ellis

Bible Reading: Luke 18:1

"And He spake a parable unto them to this end, that men ought always to pray and not to faint."

—Luke 18:1

My wife always resists speaking in public. She says that she will surely faint if she has to speak in front of a large group. On the other hand, when asked to pray in front of that same large group she will, as my pastor says, "pray heaven down." Why is that?

I have pondered this phenomenon on many occasions and have come to the realization that my wife can talk to God so easily because she knows Him so well. She is not afraid to talk to her good friend. She can tell Him her deepest thoughts without hesitation or fear because He is her best friend.

There are many verses about praying found in the Bible. Many of them are the very words of Jesus. Jesus talked to His Father from the cross with the last breath of His earthly body when He uttered, "It is finished."

My wife has taught me, through our 40 plus years together, that the power of prayer is most valuable, and we must constantly be in prayer if we are to draw closer to the Father.

Thank You, Lord, for prayer. Thank You that I can come directly to You at any time and in any place. Help me make prayer my first resort instead of making it my last resort when I am in a state of need. Help me praise You when I am in a state of joy.

Consistency or Predictability?

By M.L. Anderson

Bible Reading: Daniel 6:4

"Then the presidents and princes sought to find occasion against Daniel concerning the kingdom; but they could find none occasion nor fault; forasmuch as he *was* faithful, neither was there any error or fault found in him."

—Daniel 6:4

Almost every November, my wife and I vacation in Florida. We stay in the same town, same hotel, and we usually take the same tour boat ride on the same boat.

Captain Jack gives the narration of the waterway and the surrounding area, including the local birds, plants, and trees visible from the boat. He then pulls up close to a familiar building on shore and says, "And that pink building to your right is the famous bathhouse used in the movie *Cocoon*." Then he pauses, sets the microphone down, and slowly steers the boat back into the bay. No passengers seem impressed.

A decade ago, we wondered at what point Captain Jack would drop the infamous "bathhouse" reference. When would both crew and passengers look at each other and wonder *what in the world is he talking about? What's Cocoon?* After all, the movie was released over 30 years ago.

Well, we recently made our annual pilgrimage and guess what? It's not going to be this year that Captain Jack changes his script. He still slowed down, pulled in really close, turned down the Jimmy Buffet music, and pointed out the bathhouse to everyone on board...one more time.

Consistency is a characteristic I admire, and I believe God honors. I'm not sure if it's the same for predictability. The difference isn't often clear.

Help me, Lord, to be faithful and consistent in the things that matter most to You.

The Greatest Gift

By Gail Pallotta

Bible Reading: Isaiah 9:6–8

"For unto us a child is born, unto us a son is given: and the government shall be upon his shoulder: and his name shall be called Wonderful, Counselor, The mighty God, The everlasting Father, The Prince of Peace."

—Isaiah 9:6

When I was seven years old, my grandmother in California sent me a pair of Western boots. For Christmas, I asked my mother for a Dale Evans cowgirl skirt to go with them. Several times as Christmas grew near my mother asked, "Honey, would you be disappointed if you didn't get a Dale Evans skirt?"

Even though I really wanted the skirt, I said, "No." However, on Christmas morning, I found a brown skirt with beige fringe on the bottom and the words *Dale Evans* embroidered across it in bright red letters.

Years later, my aunt joked about the skirt in a way people do when they laugh about something that's funny only in retrospect. My mother had gone to great lengths to get that gift. After failing to find any cowgirl skirts in the local stores, she had asked several shop owners to order one. When they had said they couldn't, she had traveled sixty-five miles to buy one. Then she had found a seamstress to stitch the letters on it.

I outgrew that gift, but my mother's unselfish love endures.

In Jesus, we find the greatest gift of all. Each year without fail in this ever-changing world, Christmas proclaims God's steadfast love for us.

Dear Lord, thank You for Your unconditional love. Help me remember not only at Christmas, but all year long.

It is Well

By Judy Parrott

Bible Reading: II Kings 4:8-37

"Run now, I pray thee, to meet her, and say unto her, *Is it* well with thee? *Is it* well with thy husband? Is it well with the child? And she answered, *It is* well."

—II Kings 4: 26

It was one of those days. Every member of my family was suffering a crisis of some kind. I told several friends all the details, but I didn't feel any better. I wished I had kept my mouth shut.

Then I read this Bible story and understood the message was for me. Why did this woman tell no one—not even her husband—her child had died? Perhaps she didn't want anyone to challenge her faith and her hope for a miracle. Even when she reached Elisha, she did not tell him her son was dead. He sensed it, returned with her, and raised the child from the dead through God's power.

The story made me realize that my words have power for good or for evil. When troubles run rampant, prayer and thanksgiving to God can change the outcome. The tongue is a fire, but if it can be tamed, it can turn a situation around. If I agree with God, trust Him, and obey His Word, He will honor His Word and help me and my family.

When I began to claim God's promises and to tell Him I trusted Him to fix the problems, miracles started to happen. All of the situations were solved in a very short time.

Dear Father in heaven, I am so relieved to learn a constructive way of dealing with troubles. Thank You for teaching me to stop worrying, to speak in faith, and to wait on You for help.

Station Yourselves

By Susan M. Watkins

Bible Reading: II Samuel 23:11-12

"But he stood in the midst of the ground, and defended it, and slew the Philistines: and the Lord wrought a great victory."

—II Samuel 23:12

Man is internally conditioned for two instinctive responses to danger: fight or flight. Depending on the threat level, one or the other will be immediately engaged. Wisdom must be displayed in their respective applications. Times when the oncoming danger isn't as compelling allow for deliberate, premeditated action. The verse above records the outcome for a determined man who rebuffed the opposition and stationed himself to fight. His personal courage and fortitude earned him the honorary title of a "Mighty Man" in David's army. He was one of only three.

There are times in life when all avenues for a solution have been exhausted and the only option is to stand. Adversity is a disguised blessing. When Moses was backed up against the Red Sea and Pharaoh's army was pressing him, the situation appeared hopeless—it had the perfect ingredients for God's display of power. God is an eleventh-hour God. This ensures that we know victories come from Him and are not generated by us. We are exhorted to do all we can and then…to stand. It is a call for preparation that will usher in the power of God—a rolling-out-of-the-red-carpet for Royalty to present.

Though not governed by a clock, our Father is always on time. If you are facing enemies in your life, station yourself and defend your pea patch. Do not relinquish your land or life; the purchase price was far too costly to acquiesce. God promises to bring a great victory, while infusing the valor you already possess.

Lord, teach me what I haven't yet discovered about You and about myself.

The Value of Prayer

By Cynthia L. Simmons

Bible Reading: I Thessalonians 5:12–22

"Pray without ceasing."

—I Thessalonians 5:17

My son wore a frown as he came to me with a blue and white cup in his hand. "Mom, I don't think the dishwasher got this clean." He handed me the cup. "Here, feel it."

I took the cup and felt the outside. "You're right, Caleb. It feels like sand got glued to this cup. We'll have to wash it again."

My heart rejoiced. Caleb has had problems with sensory integration. When he was younger, he couldn't distinguish between plastic letters and the salt we immersed them in for therapy. We stimulated his skin several times a day with a soft brush and had him play in finger paint to encourage growth of the nerves. The fact that he could feel the fine grit in the cup meant that the nerves in his fingers were now functioning as they should.

I believe prayer is like that. When I spend time in prayer, my heart becomes sensitive to the guidance of the Spirit. But when I push aside prayer time to get more work done, my heart can't hear the promptings of the Spirit. All of us have sensory integration problems with our fleshly hearts. Just as I stimulated my son's hands with frequent brushing, soft clay, and finger paint, we need to stimulate our hearts constantly with prayer so we can hear the sweetness of the Spirit's voice.

"Lord, I need time with You. Prayer keeps my heart alert to Your voice. Please help me go to my knees instead of rushing off to work without Your guidance."

Remember Me

By Robert W. Ellis

Bible Reading: Numbers 10:2

"Make thee two trumpets of silver; of a whole piece shalt thou make them: that thou mayest use them for the calling of the assembly, and for the journeying of the camps."

—Numbers 10:2

The Lord told Moses to make silver trumpets to call the whole assembly of the Israelites together for the various activities of life.

It is wonderful how God uses senses to remind us of things. He uses sound, smell, sight, touch, and taste…all of the senses to bring to mind things we need to do.

As a small child growing up in a large urban area, I loved church chimes and bells. I remember stopping and listening to the lovely sounds even in the middle of important childhood activities, such as playing army or chasing the neighbor's cat.

I missed those sounds when churches stopped ringing bells or chimes. Then I moved to a house adjacent to a large church that still rang a bell and played chimes on special occasions. Even though I knew that the sound was from a digital synthesizer rather than from a real bell, the sound was still beautiful and made me stop and reminisce.

What makes you stop and think about God's Word and His promises? It might be a church bell. It might be the laugh of a child. It might be the touch of a loved one. Whatever it is, you and I should never forget the promises of God—especially the promise that He will never leave nor forsake us.

Thank You, Lord, for the ways You remind me of Your love for me. Help me be a "reminder" to someone else along the road of life.

Small Things Can Make All the Difference

By Margaret Fagre

Bible Reading: II Kings 5:1-14

"Behold also the ships, which though *they be* so great, and *are* driven of fierce winds, yet are they turned about with a very small helm, whithersoever the governor listeth."

—James 3:4

Whose life is more influential, mine or famous people on television? You know who I mean: politicians, actors, musicians, and athletes. Please do not get the wrong impression. I am happy with my life, but I would like to feel that I have some influence in the world.

The story of Naaman gives me hope for two reasons. First, through the little maid from Israel who waited on Naaman's wife. She had concern for her master, faith in a prophet of God to heal, and courage to speak up. What an impact she had in her master's life! She made the difference between his being leprous or being clean with the flesh of a little child. Sure, Naaman was a captain in the king's army, but the little maid had proof of her influence when her master was healed.

The second example was Naaman's servant. When his master's emotions were out of control with anger, he remained calm. He was wise and saw the big picture: how the Lord's ways might not seem logical, but if one wanted the blessing, one must not doubt. He gave positive encouragement in a way that Naaman could accept.

Thank You, Lord, for these examples from the scriptures. Please help me be a servant focused on Thy will and not distracted by the lives of all the celebrities. Please help me know when my small part is needed to influence my family, my friends, and my neighbors.

A Moment in Time

By June Parks

Bible Reading: John 8:12

"Then spake Jesus again unto them saying, I am the light of the world: he that followeth me shall not walk in darkness, but shall have the light of life."

—John 8:12

When I was a teen, a beautiful picture of Jesus hung in our Sunday school classroom. It was huge. I didn't know then who the artist was, but the picture was impressive.

The picture showed the long flowing robe that people often thought of Jesus as wearing, and His hair hung in gentle waves down to his shoulders. His countenance was gentle and caring and its sweetness was unmistakable. Jesus was carrying an old-fashioned lantern that appeared to be glowing brightly, and He was knocking on a heavy wooden door. I recall this famous picture of Jesus, painted by William Holman Hunt, every time I picture Him.

That picture symbolized Jesus asking for admittance into our lives. The heavy door seemed to symbolize our resistance, and the tangle of vines around the path and the door showed all of the intertwining resistance to Jesus that He had to pass through to stay on the path. But the beautiful look on Jesus' face—His peace and His enduring smile—showed that His resolve was there, and He was staying.

It was just a moment frozen in time, yet because of that wonderful old picture, I always knew that Jesus' bright lantern would be there to lighten our paths, and He would never stop seeking to gain entrance into our hearts and souls.

Dear Lord, please let me never forget that love is as close as opening the door. Help me to always have that assurance in my heart. Please grant me Your love and continual peace.

Don't Let Go of the Word

By Charlene Elder

Bible Reading: 2 Timothy 1:7

"For God hath not given us the spirit of fear; but of power, and of love, and of a sound mind."

—II Timothy 1:7

It was just a normal mammogram checkup at the doctor. Things seemed fine until they told me to come back for an ultrasound. They had spotted something on the mammogram. I hadn't felt a lump and everything had always been okay, but now what?

I had a tough battle on my hands—the enemy bombarded me with *fear*. I knew if I gave in to the fear and all the thoughts that flooded my mind, I would become spiritually paralyzed. So I dug into God's Word and stood on His promises of victory and healing. I determined that God's Word would give me victory over fear.

When I returned to the doctor and had the ultrasound, I had peace and no fear. The ultrasound confirmed God's Word—everything was clear. My mind had also been set free from worry.

If the enemy tries to attack your mind with uncertainty, fear, or worry, hold up the shield of the faith and the sword of the Spirit—God's Word—and you'll have victory and peace.

Lord, help me keep Your Word foremost in my heart and mind so I can counter the attacks of fear and worry from the enemy. Thank You for giving me victory.

Quiet Time?

By Louise Flanders

Bible Reading: Psalm 5:11; Psalm 32:11; Psalm 33:3; Psalm 35:27; Psalm 47:1; Psalm 81:1; Psalm 95:1-2; Psalm 98:4; Psalm 132:9, 16

"O clap your hands, all ye people; shout unto God with the voice of triumph."
—Psalm 47:1

Each morning for years, I eagerly awaited the sound of the garage door closing and the roar of the school bus pulling away from our house, signaling that my husband had left for work and the children were on their way to school. Finally, with everyone gone, I could enjoy my devotional time. I read quietly from the Bible then knelt for a time of silent prayer.

My quiet time followed that same pattern until I began to read from the book of Psalms every day. I became aware of a reoccurring theme: Numerous verses instructed us to clap our hands and shout for joy as we praised God. Psalm 98:4 revealed that we were not only to make a joyful noise unto the Lord, but we were to make a *loud* noise. Psalm 33:3 instructed us to sing and "play skillfully with a loud noise."

Apparently, God intended for our worship to include singing, clapping, playing instruments, and even shouting for joy. Could it be that my "quiet time" did not have to be quiet?

I gradually began to incorporate hymns and praise music into my devotional time. I also found that reading God's Word aloud made it come alive and gave it new meaning.

God is honored when we quietly and reverently worship Him, but He has also given us the freedom to shout for joy when our hearts are overflowing with praise.

Thank You, Lord, for giving us so many different ways to worship You. Create in my heart a desire to spend time with You daily.

Hill Street Blues

By Jack G. Elder

Bible Reading: Colossians 3:18-24

"Children, obey *your* parents in all things: for this is well pleasing unto the Lord."

—Colossians 3:20

I remember vividly a time when I failed to obey my mother. It left a lasting impression on me.

When snow fell in the small town of Ashland, Oregon, that was an occasion to get the sled from its winter resting place and dust it off. My mother told me, "Sled only on the property." I obeyed, but after a few times it lost all its fun.

Then, all my friends scurried over to Hill Street. The founding fathers had aptly named the street for its steep ascent or descent as the case was. Temptation grabbed me, and I marched the short block pulling my old trusty sled.

When I reached the hilltop, Hill Street was a lot steeper than I had remembered. And being the kind of boy who liked to avoid broken limbs, I gave it a good long thought. However, the other boys were yelling about some kind of barnyard animal, so I directed my sled to the top.

I stretched out on the sled, and I was off. Wow, what a thrill. I was going down Hill Street at 200 miles an hour, and the bottom was fast approaching. A parked car loomed in my path, but my trusty sled refused to turn. I hit the car's bumper with my chin. Six stitches later, my mother reminded me that had I obeyed her, the unfortunate accident would never have happened. I still have the scar as a reminder.

Father, help me obey Your Word and avoid the lessons that disobedience brings. In failing to obey my parents, I failed to obey You.

The Lord's Unexpected Return

By Marcus Beavers

Bible Reading: Luke 12: 35-40

"Be ye therefore ready also: for the Son of man cometh at an hour when ye think not."

—Luke 12:40

The Jews' view of truth was rooted in real history. They looked back to the Creation by God and to the exodus from Egypt. Truth is not nicely balanced thoughts or evolving scientific ideas. The return of Christ will happen in real space time history, just as the Scriptures have foretold. The coming of the Son of man will be a great shock to the world of men.

Luke investigated facts before he wrote. He stressed that in the biblical books of Acts and Luke. In them, we read about Jesus' actions and those of his followers. Christ's mighty miracles and complete authority over demonic spirits and nature speak strongly about His divine nature. He also had a true human nature, though he did not have a human father. Jesus' virgin birth was miraculous.

His mission on earth was that of the long prophesied Messiah. He descended from David and was raised from the dead. As the Messiah or Christ, Jesus paid the penalty for my sin against a holy God by His substitutionary, atoning sacrifice on the cross.

We find Jesus' own words about His promised return in the book of Luke. It will be a sudden and unexpected return; but for those who believe God and wait for Christ's coming, it will be a time of great change, joy, and excitement—like the excitement before a great wedding.

Oh God of Truth, I'm fully persuaded Your promises are true. On that great day of change and refreshing, I will be rejoicing. Help me now, as I press on in this fallen world.

Sunday Dinner

By Pam I. Barnes

Bible Reading: Galatians 5:13-15

"For all the law is fulfilled on one word, *even* in this; Thou shalt love thy neighbor as thyself."

—Galatians 5:14

I ran into a dear friend from the past, and we visited for hours, talking as if we'd never lost touch. It had been almost twenty years since I'd seen her, and it was nice to chat with her. I could see her eyes light up as we reminisced about our families getting together for Sunday dinner.

In the South, you understand, lunch is dinner and dinner is supper, so Sunday dinner followed immediately after church. The hostess hoped the guests would chat on the church steps long enough to allow her ample time to get home, fry chicken, and prepare special dishes and sweet tea to be served with perfection.

As my friend moved from sharing about by-gone days to sharing more recent events in her life, I watched the light in her eyes go dim. I realized she had become bitter. Two divorces and numerous conflicts with family members and friends had left her totally alone. No one called or asked her to Sunday dinner anymore.

She'd kept her chin up and maintained the good life—church attendance, a nice job, and other worthy milestones—but my heart ached for her. I began to pray for her and to ask Got to help her learn to forgive. I continue to pray daily for her to have freedom in her future and peace in her heart.

Dear Heavenly Father, please help me find a way through Your love to forgive those who have hurt me or wronged me. Only when I forgive can I truly love others as You ask me to. Please help me bless others with Your sweet peace.

Encounters of the Personal Kind

By Charlene Elder

Bible Reading: Psalm 8:1-9

"When I consider thy heavens, the work of thy fingers, the moon and the stars, which thou hast ordained; What is man, that thou art mindful of him? And the son of man, that thou visitest him?"

—Psalm 8:3-4

A Kansas farmer didn't have time for God, thinking God was not concerned about him. His wife attended church, but he didn't.

One Sunday evening while his wife was at church, a storm approached. Sirens warned people to take shelter. He hoped his wife and others would be safe in the church basement.

As the man unlocked the doors to his underground shelter near the barn, he heard loud squawking. He turned and saw ducks flopping futilely back and forth attempting to take off in the high winds.

The man, not wanting the ducks to die, hurriedly opened the barn door for them. But they were afraid and wouldn't go in. Finally, he could wait no longer and entered the shelter, reluctantly closing the door. When the all-clear signal sounded, he cautiously opened the doors, wondering what would be left of his house and barn. To his amazement, both were still standing, and the ducks, huddled under small shrubs near the barn, were safe.

He ran into the barn, grabbed what he thought ducks would eat, and scattered it in front them. They ate every piece, quacked loudly as if to say 'thank you,' and took flight.

The man watched until they were out of sight. Then, the revelation of God's love overwhelmed him. He fell to his knees in gratitude.

Lord, forgive me for sometimes thinking that You didn't care. I know You do care and You love me. Help my faith and trust in You grow stronger daily.

A Jot or a Tittle

By June Parks

Bible Reading: Matthew 5:17-19

"For verily I say unto you, Till heaven and earth pass, one jot or one tittle shall in no wise pass from the law, till all be fulfilled."

—Matthew 5:18

A jot or a tittle—do you remember hearing those funny words? When I was a kid and first heard my Bible School teacher say *a jot or a tittle*, I and my whole class laughed heartily. We repeated the phrase often for about a week.

But think how important a jot or a tittle can be. The dictionary describes those words generally as minor things—as small things. But both words can change the meaning of a sentence by their use or their absence. In advertising, for instance, small dots called bullets used in front of a sentence give emphasis. They get your attention.

Writers are taught in "grammar help" classes how important a simple comma or a period can be. Sometimes an entire meaning is distorted or lost by the misplacement or absence of a comma or a period. Even the simplest items can grow to be major. A jot (a period) or a tittle (a line signifying a dash or an exclamation point) seems bigger when we think how it can change things.

I have always loved those two words. They are significant to me. On days when I feel insignificant in this big world I live in, I consider the jot and the tittle and how they can change things. When minor things are given a chance, how major they can become.

Dear Lord, please help me be aware that in my little spot on earth I am a big, significant being. I mean something to You and to others. Let me know that I am meaningful.

Springs of Living Water

By Louise Flanders

Bible Reading: John 4:5-15, 7:37

"But whosoever drinketh of the water that I shall give him shall never thirst; but the water that I shall give him shall be in him a well of water springing up into everlasting life."

—John 4:14

As a child growing up in Texas, I looked forward each summer to visiting my grandparents in Alabama. I enjoyed time with my relatives and had also formed a friendship through the years with a girl about my age that lived nearby.

My grandparents lived in a small town, and my friend and I had a favorite spot in the center of town—an artesian well that had been there as long as I could remember.

After playing hard all morning, we would race downtown to see who could arrive at the well first. Hot and perspiring, we quenched our thirst and refreshed our spirits with the cold, clear water from the well.

As an adult, I am still drawn to that well whenever I visit my relatives. It reminds me of Jesus' words to the woman at the well in Samaria. He told her that anyone who drank the water from that well would be thirsty again, but that the water He supplied would satisfy her forever, and she would never thirst again.

Like that artesian well, Jesus is our fountain, springing forth with everlasting life. In John 7:37, Jesus says to all who are spiritually thirsty, "come unto me and drink." He is the only One who can quench our thirst and give us everlasting life.

Father, thank You that when I am spiritually dehydrated You fill my cup and restore my soul. Help me come before You daily for Your never-ending supply of spiritual water.

You Need a Friend

By Robert W. Ellis

Bible Reading: 1 Chronicles 27:33

"Ahithophel was the king's counselor: Hushai the Archite was the king's companion."

—I Chronicles 27:33

As you read through the Bible and get to Chronicles, please don't go to sleep reading the genealogy lists. When you read through the long list of names that you cannot pronounce, you may find some real jewels hidden among them. I had that experience recently.

I was plodding along reading the lists of rulers, officials, and officers who served King David, when I came to the name Hushai. He was simply listed as the "king's companion or friend."

I wondered why he was listed along with all those important officials. Then I thought, *even kings need friends*. I backed up and read more about Hushai; about how he had mourned with David and had prayed for him when he had to flee Jerusalem. We all need friends like that.

How do you acquire such a friend? Some people have a difficult time making true friends or being one. I suppose the most important aspect of friendship is trust. Do you trust others with your deepest secrets? Would they trust you with theirs?

When the lame man was brought to Jesus, he had to be lowered through the roof by his friends. Jesus was so impressed that He said, "Friend, your sins are forgiven." Since the man and his friends had trusted Jesus that much, not only did the man get to walk; his sins were forgiven as well.

Jesus can be our best friend if we, like the lame man, will only trust Him and spend time with Him.

Lord, let me be a true friend to others as You are a true friend to me.

We Are Sojourners

By Patty Rocco

Bible Reading: 1 Peter 2:11-12

"Dearly beloved, I beseech *you* as strangers and pilgrims, abstain from fleshly lusts, which war against the soul."

—I Peter 2:11

I often forget that this world is not my home. I desire comfort and engage in activities that war against my soul. (For the Christian, church work may become the thing that wars against the soul.) When I fear that I will lose something, I concentrate more on the created thing than on the Creator. I lose focus.

I love God's Word because it reminds me of who I am and where I belong. I relate to Peter because the Gospels expose his humanity. His letters, written later in his life, reveal how God transformed him. Aside from being canon, Peter's words impact me because the issues he exhorts me to consider in my life are the same issues he struggled with. Sometimes, it is fear that draws me away from God. Like Peter, I sometimes fear what others may think.

Accepting what God says about Himself and my relationship to Him is essential Christianity. I do not want to forget that my relationship to Jesus is God's priority. Therefore, I desire to immerse myself all the more in His Word and focus my love upon the Audience of One.

Thank You, Lord, for the freedom to worship You. You are the only One I am required to please. Thank You, Holy Spirit, for whispering reminders that this is not my home, I am only passing through.

Unseen Protection

By Cynthia L. Simmons

Bible Reading: Luke 22:28–34

"And the Lord said, Simon, Simon, behold, Satan hath desired *to have* you that he might sift *you* as wheat: But I have prayed for thee, that thy faith fail not..."

—Luke 22:31-32

Satan hated Simon Peter. Although Satan detests all of God's children, he probably picked Simon Peter to torture because of his close relationship with Christ. Jesus knew the abuse Satan had prepared and compared it to grinding wheat into fine powder. Just thinking of that imagery makes me cringe.

If you remember Job's story, you know that Satan can't hurt one of God's children without His consent. In Peter's case, God must have given Satan permission to test Simon Peter. However, Jesus knew Satan's scheme and went to the Father in prayer. When Jesus prays, God listens.

Later that evening after Jesus' arrest, Simon Peter, fearing for his life, denied three times that he knew Jesus. He didn't lose his faith, however, because he later repented of his sin.

In Revelation, John described Satan as the 'accuser of our brethren.' Can you imagine what Satan would like to do to us? Sometimes I worry that I haven't covered enough potential problems in my prayers. The Savior, however, protects us from tragedies we can't even imagine. When we get to Heaven, maybe Jesus will tell us all the evil He kept us from having to face. Isn't it a wonderful blessing that we don't have to mention every calamity or every nightmare in our prayers?

Dear Lord Jesus, thank You for interceding for me. Help me remember Your protection so I won't be afraid.

Higher Learning

By Susan M. Watkins

Bible Reading: Psalms 32:8-10

"I will instruct thee and teach thee in the way which thou shalt go: I will guide thee with mine eye."

—Psalm 32:8

Wisdom and knowledge are God's keys to open locked doors in our lives. Solomon spent years pursuing a lofty education and penning his thesis in Proverbs and Ecclesiastes. The Queen of Sheba was breathless after their encounters.

As a child, I struggled educationally. I spent more time standing at the back of the class than seated at my desk. My mother achieved sainthood for her heroic efforts in my success. Her patience, driven by love, became the precursor to my higher education.

God promises each of us a "Master's Degree" if we submit to His instruction. He's promised to share His secrets with us, but we must decide what type of student we will become. A bit and bridle aren't accessories I'd welcome into my wardrobe. Granted, they make quite the statement, but not the type I'd embrace publicly.

I've learned that wisdom dictates poise, regardless of the trial I'm facing. The Lord will faithfully lead me, for He alone can see the end from the beginning. Like my mother, His sole motivation is His love toward me. When examining me on the material He's taught, His silence grants an opportunity for me to reach within and extract the wisdom I've acquired. Teachers remain quiet when students are reviewed, mirroring God's behavior during our tests. God allows "retakes" until we pass—without detrimental grades. He leaves an instructive part of Himself within us to carry for life. If we consider a higher education for ourselves, we could just leave someone breathless.

Thank You for teaching me the wisest path for my life and for keeping Your eye fastened to my steps.

Never Fear Bad News

By Louise Flanders

Bible Reading: John 14:27; II Timothy 1:7; I Peter 5:7

"He shall not be afraid of evil tidings: his heart is fixed, trusting in the Lord. His heart *is* established, he shall not be afraid…"

—Psalm 112:7-8a

My son had been critically ill for months, spending more time in the hospital than at home. His health problems were so numerous that his doctors recommended we take him to a teaching hospital about 300 miles away for a comprehensive evaluation.

The day before we were to leave, my heart was filled with apprehension and fear. What if they uncovered a new medical problem that we were unaware of? What if they had no answers to problems that we knew existed?

What if they could give us no hope of recovery? What if my son regressed? What if he died?

On and on the assaults came, but I had learned to fight attacks with the only weapons that were effective: God's Word and prayer. I reached for my Bible and turned to Psalm 112. Verses seven and eight seemed to have been written just for me. I accepted the fact that it did not say that nothing bad would ever happen to me, but I received great comfort from the fact that it *did* say that I did not need to worry about the future. I never needed to fear bad news if my heart was fixed on the Lord and established in His Word.

Thank You, Lord, for the comfort of Your Word. Thank You that I can bring my problems to You, knowing that You hear me when I pray. Help me trust You with each member of my family, knowing that You love them even more than I do.

Beautiful Flight — No Landing Gear

By Pam I. Barnes

Bible Reading: Psalms 54:1-7

"For he hath delivered me out of all trouble: and mine eye hath seen *his desire* upon mine enemies."

—Psalm 54:7

Flying on a recent business trip, I learned a life-lesson I will never forget. I usually choose to drive because I'm not a "good flyer." However, the unpopular enemy called "time" prevented the road trip and put me into the air.

On the way to my destination, everything that could go wrong with a flight did go wrong. My luggage was delayed,—thankfully only by hours instead of being totally lost—my seat did not have a decent view, and we experienced extreme turbulence.

On my return trip home, I boarded the plane with all the optimism I could muster.

The day was gorgeous with the bluest sky imaginable and clouds like cotton. My view was from the most comfortable window seat, and the seat next to me was empty. All was well with me—the flight and the whole world—as far as I could tell. Then the pilot announced a landing gear malfunction.

Searching through my wallet, I found pictures of my family and friends and my eyes filled with tears. I thought of unfinished tasks, unwritten letters, and overdue phone calls I might never make. I observed the crew and other passengers and the smiles were gone from their faces. I began to pray, and I prayed a lot.

Long story short, we eventually landed smoothly. I realized that all things could be perfect in the air, but you still had to land.

Dear Lord, thank You for Your protection, which allows me to "land" and enjoy sweet peace. Help me trust You so I will have "peace on earth as it is in heaven."

When the Rain Falls, the Creeks Rise

By Margaret Fagre

Bible Reading: Proverb 16:32; Psalm 55:16-17

"He that is slow to anger is better than the mighty; and he that ruleth his spirit than he that taketh a city."

—Proverb 16:32

I grew up in southern California, the land of little rainfall. Everyone there had a lawn sprinkler system. When I moved to Baton Rouge, Louisiana, there were no sprinkler systems. There was plenty of water from natural rainfall. The water was at ground level, so when rainstorms came they flooded the low-lying areas.

Storms often raged outside our home, and storms raged inside our home as well. They were the same storms that most families face—financial crises, health issues, strained relationships, and difficult situations in raising children.

The city of New Orleans, a Louisiana city below sea level, had a pumping system that ran continually to pump the water out of the city. I needed something to pump the frustration out of my system.

I found that running prayer pumps morning, noon, and night helped remove frustration out of my life. When my anger was not near the surface, it took a lot longer to overflow, so I was slower to anger.

Thank You, Lord, for prayer. Thank You that I can reach You at any time. Thank You that You can hear my voice and drain my anger away. Please help me be slow to anger, for I have much to be calm and peaceful about in my life.

WHERE ARE YOU?

By Susan M. Watkins

Bible Reading: Genesis 3: 8-11

Genesis 3:9, "And the Lord God called unto Adam, and said unto him, Where art thou?"

—Genesis 3:9

Sometimes we misplace our integrity. After careful excavation, we find it in the bottom drawer of compromise, underneath and behind hidden motives. Its discovery often causes us to avoid God and disrupts our relationship with Him.

God's omnipotence locates us. Our Shepherd faithfully calls for His sheep. To the guilty, standing at a distance, God poses the question, "Where are you?"

Often, we fail to realize that when God asks a question He's not seeking information. The question is designed to initiate self-awareness. Where are we? Are our hearts and hands clean? God cannot leave us in our helpless condition, or He would contradict His nature. He always provides solutions to our problems.

Adam fell, and the Lord immediately responded. The solution covered Adam's vulnerability, but the sturdy animal skins sewn by God to veil man's disbelief would require a permanent canopy. The crucifixion was tightly laced within the royal birth announcement—our invitation to eternal forgiveness.

Note that God didn't point a condemning finger at man. Conversely, man didn't go looking for God. Man's choice was to hide himself. It's the unquestionable love of God that sends Him into the driving storm man generates and causes Him to cup His nail-scarred hands and call for the lost. He won't stop until the lamb is gently hoisted to His neck and carried to safety.

If God queries your position, take inventory. Open your hidden drawers and discard the useless. What formerly fit, no longer does; it clutters needed space. Answer if He calls your name so He can rescue you.

Father, give me the courage to see what I must so I can accurately reflect You.

What'll You Have?

By Robert Ellis

Bible Reading: Joshua 24:14-16

"And if it seem evil unto you to serve the Lord, choose you this day whom ye will serve; whether the gods which your fathers served that *were* on the other side of the flood, or the gods of the Amorites, in whose land ye dwell: but as for me and my house, we will serve the Lord."

—Joshua 24:15

There is a fast food restaurant in our town that puts extreme emphasis on the term *fast*. The folks behind the counter are trained to receive and fill an order in less than a minute or two.

A few years back, I was in line at that restaurant behind a short, older gentleman in a little straw hat. When it came the man's turn to place an order, the server loudly and repeatedly made his signature request, "What'll you have?" The older gentleman seemed rattled and stared at the server for a few seconds (which is an eon in the fast food world) and then asked, "Do you have a menu?" The server became agitated that his rhythm had been interrupted. "Menu? Menu? There's the menu!" he shouted at the man, as he pointed to the list of food items on the wall behind him.

Many times we are asked to make split second decisions concerning our choices or actions. We should always reflect on the possible outcome(s) of our choices by looking at God's *menu* in the scriptures to see if our choices will glorify Him.

Help me, Lord, to always be ready to make good choices in life. If I feel rushed or pushed in a wrong direction, let me focus on You before I make my choice.

Stand Fast in Your Liberty

By Judy Parrott

Bible Reading: Galatians 4:29-Galatians 5:1

"Stand fast therefore in the liberty wherewith Christ hath made us free, and be not entangled again with the yoke of bondage."

—Galatians 5:1

Jonathan Swift wrote *Gulliver's Travels* in 1726. Gulliver, shipwrecked on an island, was rescued after nine years. Upon returning home, doctors locked him in an asylum because he raved about his unbelievable adventures in a miniature world of Lilliputians. His wife and son, however, believed the Lilliputians were real.

Gulliver failed to convince a judge of his sanity, so guards shackled him and began to haul him away. Just in time, his son burst into the courtroom with an object in a box he had found with his father's possessions. The boy emptied the small box onto a table, and out jumped a tiny sheep—living evidence of the beings Gulliver had tried to describe. *Gulliver walked out a free man.*

When a person shares with us something he or she believes in, we owe it to him or her to listen without judging. If we are humble, we may learn some valuable lessons. One lesson is that with God all things are possible.

Have you ever been doubted? If you know the truth, do not waver, but stand firm in spite of persecution. In due time, God promises to exalt you—here on earth or in heaven.

Thank You, Awesome Father, for revealing truth to me through the Word of God. Give me boldness to share it in love.

The View From Within

By Susan M. Watkins

Bible Reading: I Samuel 16:6-11

"But the Lord said unto Samuel, Look not on his countenance, or on the height of his stature; because I have refused him: for *the Lord seeth* not as man seeth; for man looketh on the outward appearance, but the Lord looketh on the heart."

—I Samuel 16:7

The Father's eyes—penetrating vision that scans the landscape of man. He is not influenced by our exteriors, despite His painstaking design in forming them. No, His eyes are connected to holiness, causing Him to search earnestly for this attribute in His creation. Easily located by Him, it moves Him to act and releases our destiny.

Our hearts are the only organs that communicate accurately with Him. They house the abundance of who we are and hold our dreams and desires. They also balance our motives. They become the spiritual scales and thermometers of our progress. God views the conditions therein and responds.

Eternal gratitude is stored in my heart for God's uncompromised justice. When others misjudge, He doesn't. I can lie down in His lush pasture, knowing if mankind misunderstood, He did not. He didn't look on my form, but at what rhythmically beats between my shoulders sustaining my life. I can only worship at His feet in the embrace of His pure evaluations. In undying loyalty, my heart aligns in concert with His and proclaims His worthiness. I cannot surrender this privilege to mere rocks and extend an invitation for your heartfelt participation.

Lord, give me a heart like Yours, so I can be effectively used to create a longing for You in others.

The Glory of His Light

By Judy Becker

Bible Reading: Proverbs 20:27; John 1:1-9

"For thou wilt light my candle: the Lord my God will enlighten my darkness."
—Psalm 18:28

Ponder the power of natural light. God reveals the design and beauty of the whole universe through it; all life flourishes by the energy from it; and no amount of darkness can resist it. The light, however, that ignites our candle is special spiritual light, an ability to see the things of God, enlightened by the Holy Spirit. The candle—our spirit—glows brighter and brighter as long as we keep receiving His light.

The source, the "Father of Lights," shines through Jesus, "the Light of the World;" hence through Christ we become the dispensers of His light *in* this world. It is not automatic, but depends upon our exposure to His Word.

In scripture, light typifies truth and understanding, because light reveals. Paul prays that we might all receive the light of "the spirit of wisdom and revelation in the knowledge of him [Jesus]" (Eph. 1:17) "in whom are hid all the treasures of wisdom and knowledge" (Col. 2:3). As we read His Word, He lights our darkness, and we in turn light the way for the unsaved by that truth.

When we publicly put our "light" on a lamp stand, it illuminates the whole house. Jesus calls us the "children of light." We are destined for the "city of light." The more of this light we reflect, the more we glorify Him. At the end, Jesus said, "Then shall the righteous shine forth as the sun in the kingdom of their Father" (Matthew 13:43).

Lord, may I ever seek Your light, that the world may see that light in me and glorify You, even as *I* glorify You by it.

Oh, Happy Day

By Jack Elder

Bible Reading: Psalm 118:22-24

"This is the day *which* the Lord hath made; we will rejoice and be glad in it."
—Psalm 118:24

This is your day. How can you be sure? Verse 24 of Psalm 118 says so. God created this day for you. The Lord didn't make it as a random act of chance. Today is a special day designed by the Creator of heaven and earth. This very day is the one the Lord set aside for this particular date. Yesterday is gone. Tomorrow is only a hope. You have today to accomplish the purposes God designed for you to accomplish today.

Maybe you didn't wake up with a great attitude. Perhaps you were down on life, saying things like, "same old things—different day." However it started, God made this day for you.

That thought alone should generate a positive response. In fact, the psalmist said you should rejoice and be glad. The word "rejoice" means to spin around excitedly. You should be so joyful you can't sit still for the fact that this is your day.

Not only should you rejoice, but you should also be glad. All day long, you can be glad. Let the corners of your mouth curl up into a smile, and walk with a cheerful disposition. Nothing can get in your way today because the Lord made this day for you.

There are no "what ifs." The verse does not say, "if all things are going excellently then rejoice and be glad." Rejoice and be glad because creation waited for this very day. This is the day.

Thank You, Father, for this day You made for me.

Dialing 9-1-1...Answering 9-1-1

By Pam I. Barnes

Bible Reading: Psalms 86:1-7

"In the day of my trouble I will call upon thee: for thou wilt answer me."
—Psalm 86:7

We are all familiar with the emergency number "9-1-1." If we haven't placed a call ourselves, we've seen how it works on television or in the movies. It has also been a news topic from time to time when people question 9-1-1 response time.

But how is it on the "answering" side of the 9-1-1 call? When we dial in, we may be scared or panicked. Yet we know the person on the other end of the phone needs the address right away in order to dispatch help. We probably do a less than perfect job in providing the pertinent information, yet we expect and demand a quick response and adequate help.

I thought about my prayer life and wondered if that was how I prayed. I realize I need to pray often to God to build a relationship with Him, sharing my casual life experiences and not just praying when I am involved in a crisis. I need to have faith in my Lord and give Him the whole problem when I call out in prayer. Then I simply need to trust Him to handle things as only He can.

Dear Lord, thank You for always listening to my prayers. Thank You for being there for me 24/7 and for answering my "emergency calls" as well as my daily prayers. Please give me the peace of knowing I can give You my troubles, and You will always handle them for me. All I need is faith in You, my loving Father.

Hope

By Charlene Elder

Bible Reading: Jeremiah 31:17

"And there is hope in thine end, saith the Lord, that thy children shall come again to their own border."

—Jeremiah 31:17

There was little hope of finding our daughter, Ange. We hadn't heard from her for over three days—long, hard days. The police told us there wasn't much they could do, since she was 18 and old enough to be on her own. *Would turning in a missing persons report help us locate her?*

We didn't know what to do but pray. I found a scripture in Jeremiah that spoke volumes of hope to me. God's Word told me there was hope; that my daughter would come again to her own border (house). I reminded the Lord each morning of that scripture and His promise, and I continued to pray for my daughter's safety.

Four days later, the phone rang. It was our daughter. She was safe, but in another state with a crazy bunch of people. She begged us not to do anything because they would kill her. I made her promise to call each week, or I'd go to the police. She faithfully called each week, and I continued to pray.

Within three months, Ange was back home, miraculously delivered from the pit of hell. She is now the happy mother of three precious young children—my grandchildren.

When situations appear to be hopeless with your children, the Lord will give you hope as you trust in Him.

Lord, You know where my children are and what they need. You are the only One who can touch their hearts and bring them back. Thank You for the promises of Your Word and for Your faithfulness.

Freedom of Choice

By Susan M. Watkins

Bible Reading: Jeremiah 29:4-7, 11

"Build ye houses, and dwell in them; and plant gardens, and eat the fruit of them."

—Jeremiah 29:5

Captivity appears in numerous forms. The hands and feet need not be bound to make one a prisoner. A delayed promotion, a prodigal child, a financial impasse, a faltering marriage, or health issues all present challenges.

The good news is that God wants and expects us to continue with our lives in spite of adversity! He calls us to adjust our outlook, taking our eyes off the limits and experiencing love and joy on a daily basis. We are even challenged to multiply in our hardships.

It's easy to focus on everything that's wrong, but to locate the jewels in our lives requires careful searching. God's Word is our roadmap to a successful journey, but we must choose to sharpen our vision. Trusting Him grants us the ability to increase in even the most adverse circumstances. He additionally calls upon us to pray for those who appear to be our taskmasters. God knows humanity's playing field is globally leveled.

There is only one Shepherd whose love for us is unfathomable; He even knows our hair count. We can relax under His credible Shepherd's hook. All is precisely on schedule for our lives, and we know our captivity has a definite end.

Lord, open my eyes and heart to realize—regardless of what I see—that I walk in complete freedom and victory under Your capable care.

Gramps

By M.L. Anderson

Bible Reading: Psalm 127:3

"Lo, children are an heritage of the Lord: and the fruit of the womb is his reward."

—Psalm 127:3

My family called him Charlie Lager. I called him "Gramps," but not often enough. He was my great grandfather.

Gramps looked old through my little eyes. He was bald with the same pattern I'm destined for today. He wore plaid shirts with suspenders, and his glasses were always dusty. My memories are few, but I know he loved me.

I've heard them all before: stories about his Minnesota life, his four daughters, the homestead across the Mississippi in Wisconsin, making crocks at the pottery, the Saturday night rowboat trips to downriver dance halls, the premature death of his son and later his wife. I've walked in places where he walked, and I've stood over his stone at the cemetery.

I wish I had a time machine so I could travel back and observe his daily life. It might have been fascinating or sad, surprising or disappointing.

Today, this man is a legend and the anchor of the rag-tag extended family that shares the Lager heritage. We celebrate him, yet each generation remembers him less. Old photos are pawed over and tales are embellished. Facts are difficult to separate from myths.

Was he a righteous man? Did he consider himself a good father? Did he have faith in God? In our minds we build him into who we want him to be—a hero; and after all the tales are told, what's wrong with that?

Father, help me make my life a legacy of honor to You. Let it be said by my children that I was a righteous man.

Moses: Servant of God and Psalm Writer

By Marcus Beavers

Bible Reading: Psalm 90

"For we are consumed by thine anger, and by thy wrath we are troubled. Thou hast set our iniquities before thee, our secret *sins* in the light of thy countenance."

—Psalm 90:7-8

Moses' Psalm, written over 3500 years ago, is a poignant reminder of man's tragic fall into sin. The world and man are now abnormal, not as they were originally made by our loving Creator. Sin and death, sickness and disease, hatred and war were never a part of God's original, perfect creation.

Moses finds hope in the Lord's mercy. The Lord has been a dwelling place in all generations because He has been a place of shelter for those who have believed and obeyed Him. In another scripture, Moses writes: "The eternal God is your refuge, and underneath are the everlasting arms."

Psalm 90 emphasizes God's wrath against sin and what it has done to mankind and the relationships of His creatures. He is the infinite, personal God who is good. He spoke into existence a vast creation which fits together in a rational way. He thought, acted, felt, and used language in the beginning to create via His powerful Word.

Moses was inspired by God to write the first five books of the Bible. The Bible's central message is about the promised Messiah. On the Mount of Transfiguration, Moses and Elijah were permitted to speak with and to encourage Christ about the importance of His redemptive work. Jesus completed that work that we might be complete in Him.

Holy, Loving God, help me understand Your Word. Thank You for Your created order and beauty in the world. I need to know Your truth. Help me read and study the Bible often.

The Guiding Candle

By Pam I. Barnes

Bible Reading: Psalms 27:1-5

"The Lord is my light and my salvation; whom shall I fear? the Lord is the strength of my life; of whom shall I be afraid?"

—Psalm 27:1

On a recent trip to the coast, I was able to tour a mighty lighthouse. As I viewed the structure, I realized the importance and uniqueness of this building and of all lighthouses. Some have waves constantly beating their foundation and their location may be lonely and desolate, and yet they serve well as guiding lights when people are in the dark and possibly lost in the waters.

A dedicated ship captain would not be able to keep a candle burning consistently in any boat. He might try, but it would be treacherous at best and the hours too long. The candle would not be safe from the elements; wind and water would constantly put out the flame.

The still and stable lighthouse serves with strength and position. It sits on the edge of potential danger, and it sits on the edge of safety. Someone must tend this great fortress and make sure its light is burning every night. Those who are lost only need to look for the lighthouse and trust it to mark their way to safety. Those caring for the lighthouse fulfill their job by keeping the light burning so the lighthouse can serve its purpose.

My dear Savior, thank You for being my lighthouse and offering Your light to me. I will look for it and trust it to guide me safely home. When You ask me to be a lighthouse to lead people to You, please give me strength to handle the duty and to have faith in You so that my light shines brightly.

Knowledge and Freedom

By Charlene Elder

Bible Reading: Hosea 4

"My people are destroyed for lack of knowledge: ..."

—Hosea 4:6a

Crippled by a continual anxiety disorder, Susan could not gain victory in her daily life. Any time she heard bad news—whether from the media or from family or friends—her mind instantly thought of the "what if" scenario. Susan went to church regularly, but wondered if she was losing her mind because she couldn't overcome the anxiety and fear.

It wasn't until Susan received Christian counseling that she began to understand how Satan's trap of fear, worry, and anxiety had caught and held her. She learned how to overcome his attacks by standing on God's Word for her deliverance instead of worrying and becoming fearful or anxious. Susan continued to gain victory over fear, worry, and anxiety, and it wasn't long before she was teaching others the importance and the power of God's Word in their daily lives.

The Lord told the prophet Hosea, "My people are destroyed for lack of knowledge." (Knowledge of God's Word and His power in them to overcome the world and the enemy). God's Word is still the same today and will be the same tomorrow.

When we face times of attack from the enemy, we need to dig into God's Word like Susan did. As we do, our faith will deepen, and we will become spiritually stronger.

Lord, help me when I become fearful. I know that You are bigger than anything I will encounter, so I don't need to worry. I will use Your Word to counter the attacks of the enemy.

Words of Life

By Judy Parrott

Bible Reading: John 6:40-51

"And this is the will of him that sent me, that every one which seeth the Son, and believeth on him, may have everlasting life: and I will raise him up at the last day."

—John 6:40

Alicia never told anyone in the trailer park that she was a well-known evangelist back in Mexico. She just spoke to those around her with love saying, "God bless you," or "God loves you." The downcast neighbors rarely lifted their heads to look at her; but one night a pickup truck drove right into her yard and stopped. Alicia ran out. The driver sat in the seat weeping loudly.

The driver said, "I want to kill my neighbor!"

Alicia prayed quickly, *what do I say, Lord?* Then she spoke to the man, "Did you give this man life? Why would you want to kill him? Change your mind right now and pray with me if you want to change."

The man prayed, "Yes, I want God. Come into my heart."

Alicia said, "Now say, 'I am free.'"

The man obeyed. Immediately, Alicia went with him to tell the man he forgave him. His neighbor and the neighbor's entire family accepted Jesus. All were baptized in water and the Spirit. This was a major breakthrough.

The man in the truck now has a call on his life to become a pastor.

Dear Lord, help me hear Your voice in difficult situations. I need the mind of Christ to help people in crisis. I can do nothing without You. Thank You for everlasting life and the love You give me for people. It all comes from You.

Desires of Your Heart

By Bonnie Greenwood Grant

Bible Reading: Mathew 7:7-11

"If you then, being evil, know how to give good gifts unto your children, how much more shall your Father which is in heaven give good things to them that ask him?"

—Matthew 7:11

My three-year-old son, Jeremy, threw Candy, our seventeen-year-old Siamese cat into the trash compacter, closed the drawer, and pushed the button. Our daughter, Becky, ran to find her dad and me, yelling, "Jeremy threw Candy into the trash compacter. I'm too afraid to open the drawer."

Kerry and I ran to the kitchen, and Kerry opened the drawer. Candy was alive, meowing softly. A large uncrushed bottle had saved her life. Kerry gently lifted her out, laid her on the floor, and called a vet. I found a box, and we laid her in it, put her in the car, and raced to the vet's.

X-rays showed her pelvis was crushed. The vet said she probably wouldn't survive surgery because of her age.

Kerry had never been one to bother God with personal things. He believed that God existed, but that He didn't want to be bothered by human concerns. *I prayed for Candy.*

The next morning, I called the vet. "I'm calling about Candy Grant. Please say she made it."

"She came through with flying colors," was the reply. "She's walking around complaining about being here. I've never seen a faster recovery."

We danced over and brought our miracle cat home. She had pins through her pelvis for three weeks, but after their removal, she did figure eights around our feet.

Kerry rejoiced for Candy, but more for himself, as he realized the Creator of the Universe cared about him personally.

Awesome God, thank You for loving me and caring about my concerns.

Growing Through Temptation

By Dottie Frassetto

Bible Reading: James 1:12-15

"Blessed is the man that endureth temptation: for when he is tried, he shall receive the crown of life, which the Lord hath promised to them that love him."

—James 1:12

I opened the box and found not one, but three step stools. I had paid for one, not three. *It was the store's mistake,* I thought. *I'll take the extra stools back later.* One day drifted into another, and in a few weeks, all three stools were in use around my house.

Each time I unfolded a stool, my conscience stung me, but not enough to do the right thing and take them back. Three months later, I swallowed a lump of embarrassment and went to the store with my money in hand to pay for the extra stools. They refused my money saying the stools were outdated inventory. It was too late to make it right. The stools were mine; but every time I stepped on one, I was reminded that procrastination has a price.

Temptation is as much an occasion to do the right thing as it is to do the wrong thing. It involves making a choice. It provides an opportunity to develop Christ-like character. I missed my chance to grow spiritually, but I learned a valuable lesson: respond promptly when God speaks.

Lord, thank You for reminding me that my integrity is kept intact when I listen and respond to You with my choices in both the big and little things in life.

Finding Your Purpose

By Brenda Thompson Ward

Bible Reading: Colossians 3:12-17

"And whatsoever ye do in word or deed, *do* all in the name of the Lord Jesus, giving thanks to God and the Father by him."

—Colossians 3:17

Twenty-seven years ago, my husband and I entered our first church ministry. John knew what the Lord wanted him to do, but I wasn't certain what the Lord wanted from me. Therefore, I wandered through a maze of different tasks that were not really what He meant for me to do.

After working in children's church for several years, I found that I didn't work well with little children. I then served as a school librarian for fifteen years—a job I enjoyed. However, when I was asked to teach a ladies' Sunday school class, I realized that God had called me to teach. I taught that class in Alabama for twelve years, and I now teach a ladies' Bible study in our church in Georgia.

The ministries of the Lord are plenteous. There are jobs for everyone, and it is important for each of us to find our place in the ministry. If we ask, the Lord will lead us to the place of service where we are needed.

We have different talents, and each of us can find a place to serve the Lord. There will always be a need for preachers, teachers, encouragers, care givers, and prayer warriors. Simply sending a card to a person who is sick can have a great impact on them.

I'm glad the Lord revealed my place in ministry to me. I'm certain He will reveal yours.

Lord, reveal to me the place of service You have for me. I want to please You and be used for Your glory.

Lift One Another Up

By Charlene Elder

Bible Reading: Exodus 17:8-13

"But Moses hands *were* heavy; and they took a stone, and put it under him, and he sat thereon; and Aaron and Hur stayed up his hands, one on the one side, and the other on the other side; and his hands were steady until the going down of the sun."

—Exodus 17:12

Everyone needs to be encouraged from time to time; in fact, Christians are to be encouragers. Encouragers are those who give support and hope when times are tough. They pray for you and with you and stand in the gap and lift you up. Without encouragers, even believers can get discouraged with the events of life.

When the Israelites battled the Amalekites, Moses became tired and needed encouragement. When he held his hands up, as the Lord had instructed, Israel defeated the enemy. When he let them down, the enemy gained the upper hand. That's when Aaron and Hur became encouragers for Moses. They stood with him, holding his hands steady all day until the Israelites defeated the Amalekites.

I have a great friend and prayer partner who encourages me in God's Word and in prayer when I have specific prayer needs or requests. In turn, I am an encourager to her when she requests prayer. What a privilege it is to stand in the gap with a friend and fellow believer. What a privilege it is to be able to pray for one another, confident that the Lord will hear and answer.

Lord, help me to be an encourager to my family, my friends, and those I meet. Show me how I can demonstrate Your love and bless those around me.

Keep, Kept, Cooped?

By M.L. Anderson

Bible Reading: I Peter 1:5

"Who are kept by the power of God through faith unto salvation ready to be revealed in the last time."

—I Peter 1:5

My mind is filled with quirky leftover questions from my childhood whenever I hear certain phrases. For example: "My brother's keeper." When I heard that phrase, I couldn't help but think of someone who worked at a zoo babysitting his sibling.

And then there is: "Now I lay me down to sleep. I pray the Lord my soul to keep." So does God want to keep my soul while I'm sleeping? Does He keep it in a cupboard with the dishes, or does He keep it in a cage at the zoo where someone's brother works? I needed a better perspective on the word "keep."

In today's Bible reading, the passage refers to Christians, "who are kept by the power of God through faith." There's that keep-kept thing again. Does *kept* do anything for you? It grabbed me about as much as stale bubblegum.

Modern Bible translations offered other English words like guarded, protected, and shielded in place of *kept*. When I read it again and substituted one of those words, I gained a better understanding of what God's telling me.

Beyond the passage, I now know *kept* can also mean guarded, protected, and shielded. My brother's keeper means his protector. Now when my head hits the pillow at night, and I think, *now I lay me down to sleep…* I'll take extra comfort in knowing He's guarding, protecting, and shielding my soul from the enemy.

Lord, help me understand Your Word and Your Words better so that I might know You better and know what You expect from me.

Carved in the Palm of His Hand

By Bonnie Greenwood Grant

Bible Reading: Isaiah 49:15-16

"Behold, I have graven thee upon the palms of *my* hands."

—Isaiah 49:16a

I have a full-sized carousel horse in my living room—a big, black stallion with four white stockings, a white blaze on his face, and a billowing mane. It took me over a year to carve him at the carousel carving school in Chattanooga, Tennessee. Every week, I drove an hour and forty-five minutes from Acworth, Georgia to Chattanooga and stayed over night so I'd have two days to carve.

The pattern for each body part was traced onto the bass wood boards, cut out with a band saw, and glued together. Wood chip by wood chip, my horse came to life. The head, neck, legs, and tail went pretty fast, but the body slowed me down. The trappings were very detailed, and I hate detail. Finally, my horse was painted and brought home. It took four men to help me get him off the truck.

One day as I was hurrying out the door, I glanced at my horse. The sunlight reflected off him, and I couldn't resist going into the living room and hugging him. I looked down at his beautiful face and thought *I can't believe I carved you. How could I have made something so lovely?* Without thinking, I kissed him on the forehead and left the house.

As the door closed, I realized that God feels the same way about us. Though others will forget us, the One that created us, will not; He has carved us in the palm of His hand.

Father, thank You for loving me and for keeping me and those I love safe in the palm of Your hand.

The Problem of Patience

By Bill Larmore

Bible Reading: Exodus 14:13-14

"The Lord shall fight for you, and you shall hold your peace."

—Exodus 14:14

Long ago, 600,000 Israelites—escapees from Egyptian slavery—were camped by the Red Sea. They were hungry, frightened, and questioning God. The pillar of smoke by day and the column of fire by night were great acts, but what had God done for them lately? And Moses? Some leader he was. They needed to cross the sea, but he seemed to just be waving at the water.

Even worse, company had come to dinner. Pharaoh of Egypt and his entire cavalry had arrived to chase them back to Egypt. For Israel, it was give up or drown.

Moses probably thought, "I'll fight," only to realize he could not. He had no army, only a dependant mob. He despaired of his own devices and reached out to God, begging Him to intervene. God, as always, responded with a powerful, perfect solution to the problem. Moses and the Israelites walked across the sea on dry land. Pharaoh's cavalry tried to follow, but drowned.

Our normal first reaction to trouble may be to feel trapped and despairing. We must follow Moses' example and trust God, not ourselves. Pose the problem to Him and then wait patiently to marvel at how He will lead you to solve it. He will never disappoint you.

Dear Father God, thank You for Your infinite patience with my impatience. In my varied misfortunes, my first reaction far too often has been to feel trapped and plunge blindly ahead to escape. Please cause me, like Moses, to hold my peace and watch You provide victorious outcomes for my problems.

Father of Lies

By Bonnie Greenwood Grant

Bible Reading: Psalm 24

"Who shall ascend into the hill of the Lord? or who shall stand in his holy place? He that hath clean hands, and a pure heart; who hath not lifted up his soul unto vanity, nor sworn deceitfully."

—Psalm 24:3-4

When my son was sixteen, I overheard him on the phone telling his friend he had three pair of Cavaricci—the latest in men's slacks. When he saw my expression of disapproval, he realized I knew he only had two pair. I could tell he thought I was going to give him the "It's what you are that's important, not what you have" lecture.

Jeremy was the master of prevarication. When he was in third grade, I volunteered in his classroom. One day when I came to volunteer, the teacher ran up and hugged me. "Oh, I'm so glad you're here," she said. "Jeremy told me your house burned down with you in it." I stared at my son, who at least had the grace to act embarrassed.

I, like most people, want to feel important. I like to be respected; I want my opinion to be valued. I don't care if people envy my possessions, since possessions are replaceable. However, my character is important to me. I want to be a person of honor.

Years later, I mentioned the slacks incident to my son's friend. He laughed. "Oh, I always discounted half of everything he said," he replied. "Jeremy finally learned that I liked him because he was a good person and a good friend." I looked at my son, who met my gaze and smiled. He finally understood.

You are The Truth and The Way. Help me not to desire vain, worthless things, but to seek You alone.

NEEDS MET

By Charlene Elder

Bible Reading: Matthew 6:31-32; Matthew 10:30-31

"Therefore, take no thought saying, What shall we eat? Or, What shall we drink? Or, Wherewithal shall we be clothed?... for your heavenly Father knoweth that ye have need of all these things."

—Matthew 6:31- 32

"Fear ye not, therefore, ye are of more value than many sparrows."

—Matthew 10:31

Her house was gone. In an instant, a terrible storm had destroyed it; but she and her family were safe. They needed temporary shelter, and she found a place close to a local store. Starting over was difficult. Each morning, she had to secure food for her family.

One morning, to her surprise, she awoke to find a supply of food. There was more the next morning and the following morning. Her family was going to make it. From his window next door, the kind pet store owner smiled, knowing the mother bird and her family would be okay.

Have you ever been in a situation when you did not know how you would get money for food, rent, or other bills? Perhaps you are currently facing a time of uncertainty and lack. Be encouraged. The Lord will meet your needs. He is your provider. Don't worry, fret, or be anxious about your circumstances. Do what you can do and trust the Lord for His abundant blessings and provisions. He won't disappoint you.

Lord, help me trust You more because I know You love me. Thank You for providing what I need. I *will* trust You.

Wrinkles, Worry, and Sin

By Brenda Thompson Ward

Bible Reading: Job 16:7-8

"And thou hast filled me with wrinkles, *which* is a witness *against me*: and my leanness rising up in me beareth witness to my face."

—Job 16:8

Aging is not the only cause of wrinkles. Weather, skin type, heredity, and smoking can cause wrinkles and signs of aging, as can anger, envy, stress, and sickness.

Job's body wore away with disease and pain until he was nothing but skin and bones. His face was furrowed, not with age, but with pain and sickness. Job's discomfort was evident to all those who saw him.

Sin is a wrinkle on our souls. Others can tell when we are depressed or worried about something. Our eyes—the windows to our souls—communicate our state of mind. We don't even have to speak a single word. Our facial expressions reveal happiness, sadness, worry, and anger.

The Word of God is the remedy for the wrinkles of sin in our lives. When we launder our hearts with *living water*, the detergent of confession, and the bleach of God's forgiveness, the stain of sin is removed. When we apply the fabric softeners of prayer and the acceptance of God's forgiveness, our hearts become soft. We can even add starch for strength through the Holy Ghost.

Lord, help me guard my heart against sin. Please help me come to You when I do things that displease You. Help me come to You daily for Your forgiveness and cleansing power.

Next Someday

By M.L. Anderson

Bible Reading: James 5:3

"Your gold and silver is cankered; and the rust of them shall be a witness against you, and shall eat your flesh as it were fire. Ye have heaped treasure together for the last days."

—James 5:3

My dad was the sole survivor of the people I called parents. As the only child, I cleaned out his house after he died, rummaging through his drawers, cabinets, and closets, making split-second decisions about whether to "save" or "toss" belongings he had kept for years.

My folks never threw away much. Paper items like letters, old Valentine cards, store receipts, and yellowed newspapers abounded. As sentimental as I am, I still shredded and burned bags of papers, all the while coming to an astonishing awareness that my kids would paw through my "stuff" someday and throw away gobs of my belongings too.

So next someday, I plan to start a backyard fire early in the morning and fuel it all day long with old letters from acquaintances I barely remember, my SAT test results, grade school report cards, ticket stubs from past Atlanta Braves baseball games, and even my U.S. Marine Corps letters of commendation.

There will be few items for my kids' "toss" pile. Of course, I'll be ceremonious about it all and read each item for the last time before placing it on the fire. Then I'll raise my glass of prune juice and make a toast in my solitude. It should be a nostalgic reflective day.... next someday.

Help me, Lord, to keep my eyes on eternal treasurers and not store up things of this world.

Facing Hard Times

By Cynthia L. Simmons

Bible Reading: Romans 5:1-5

"...but we glory in our tribulations also: knowing that tribulation worketh patience; and patience, experience; and experience, hope."

—Romans 5:3b-4

I sat downstairs watching a movie with my husband and straining my ears to hear my son in the kitchen. I couldn't hear the clatter of dishes and wondered if he'd forgotten to clean the kitchen. Since he loves to play video games, I thought he might be on the computer instead of doing his chores.

Tears filled my eyes when I found him upstairs reading a book—by himself. For most kids that would not be unusual, but Caleb struggles with learning disabilities. Each small skill he has learned has been as hard as scaling a sheer cliff with ropes. I have home schooled him through some very hard times. In fact, nothing has been easy. Often when he made mistakes, he threw himself on the floor and screamed that he was stupid.

I battled frustration too. Watching my son fail over and over felt like swallowing razor blades. Desperation drove me to take special education classes and to read books on how the brain works. I learned to celebrate even the tiniest improvements and never gave up. Teaching him changed my life. I came to understand the power of prayer as God guided us both to overcome impossible barriers. The rough times made me turn to God, and I now understand His grace better.

Lord, please help me as I face hard times. Teach me and guide me so I will grow. In the midst of the conflict, remind me of Your steadfast love.

Love is the Greatest

By Judy Parrott

Bible Reading: I Corinthians 13

"And now abide faith, hope, love, these three; but the greatest of these *is* love."
—I Corinthians 13:13

The dentist warned me that I had a slight crack in my front tooth. Yep, you guessed it. My whole tooth disappeared—never to be seen again—in a bite of pizza.

I quickly learned from some unpleasant situations that there is a class distinction based on the presence or absence of teeth. After enduring embarrassing stares, I went to see the play, "My Fair Lady," knowing it would be dark in the theater.

The main character, Eliza, had a Cockney accent, making her less than human to a prideful professor. He bet his associate that he could pass Eliza off as a 'lady' in six months by grooming her like one would train a dog. In his eyes, she was only low-class scum.

The professor soon came to understand that true class had more to do with a pure, honest heart than with anything else. He eventually humbled himself and admitted that he had fallen in love with Eliza and could not bear to lose her. The class barrier had dissolved.

The story revealed to me that love covers many faults. My missing tooth was not important to those who loved me. Pure love comes from God into our hearts and flows to others from there. This love is eternal; it never fails. Love *is* the greatest!

Dear Lord, what else can I do but love You back? Thank You for Your unconditional love and for sending Jesus to remove my sins 'as far as the east is from the west.'

God Doesn't Make Junk

By Brenda Thompson Ward

Bible Reading: Psalm 139

"I will praise thee; for I am fearfully and wonderfully made."

—Psalm 139:14

When I was a thirty years old, my husband and I moved to the city of Chattanooga to study for the ministry. At that time, I was very insecure and self-conscious. I would never have spoken to a group of ladies the way I do now when I teach Bible studies. In Chattanooga, I met a wonderful Christian woman who taught me a valuable lesson about who I am and who God is.

I learned that God knows every move I make, even before I make it. He knows all of my thoughts before I think them. He knows my words before I speak them. Nothing I do surprises Him, and everywhere I go, He is there. He created and understands my personality.

Had I not become acquainted with Psalm 139, I would not have been capable of accepting myself as I am. For a long time, I felt God had made a mistake when he made me loud and quick-spoken. I realize now that He gave me the personality He wanted me to have. He had a reason for that.

As God's child, I am to work to become a better Christian and to use my strengths for His glory. I must also accept my weakness and let Him become strong in me, knowing He created me and loves me as I am.

Help me, Lord, to recognize my strengths and weakness. You made me the way I am for a reason, so help me use my strengths for Your work. Help me work on my weaknesses so I can be of greater service to You.

Peace of Mind in Troubling Times

By Charlene Elder

Bible Reading: Isaiah 26:1-11

"Thou wilt keep him in perfect peace, whose mind is stayed on thee: because he trusteth in thee."

—Isaiah 26:3

I remember as a ninth grader finding out that my father had cancer. I was scared. I didn't want my daddy to die. Mom told me he would have surgery, and we were to pray, have faith, and trust the Lord.

Alone in my bedroom that night, I prayed asking the Lord not to let my daddy die. No sooner had those words come out of my mouth than an abundance of peace flooded over me like ocean waves. My entire bedroom was filled with peace. I knew that my daddy would be all right. I thanked the Lord for taking care of my daddy and continued trusting Him. Daddy came through the operation fine, and he lived a long life of 83 years.

When I am tempted to doubt God's Word or His ability to work in my life and my situation, He reminds me that He is just as faithful today as He was many years ago, and I experience the same abundance of peace

Lord, You know what is going on in my life and around me. You're my only hope and my peace. I will keep my mind focused on You and Your Word and trust You. I receive Your peace right now.

Hide the Word

By Jack G. Elder

Bible Reading: Psalm 119:9-16

"Thy word have I hid in mine heart, that I might not sin against thee."
—Psalm 119: 11

Many years ago in elementary school, I was a member of a Christian boy's club. It was military style, and I could earn ranks by memorizing scripture. It was a clever way to get boys to get in the Word and to get the Word into boys. I was always up for a challenge and began with the shortest verses and passages, mostly in the Psalms. This verse was one of the first I memorized and was one of the most important.

There were many times as I grew up that scripture came to mind when I was in a position to do something wrong. The Word reminded me to reconsider what I was about to do. The Word works deep down in the heart—its hiding place. More than just in the memory, it resides in a place where it can make changes to our lives.

The Word I memorized as a young boy built the foundation for my love of the Word. I found that it never let me down. It was always true. I still know this verse because I hid it in my heart so many years ago.

By the way, I made it to the highest rank—Master Sergeant. I hid many scriptures in my heart.

Father, help me hide Thy Word in my heart each day that I might rely on it to keep me from sinning against You.

Rainy Days, Mondays, and Certain Songs

By M.L. Anderson

Bible Reading: Psalm 32:7

"Thou art my hiding place; thou shalt preserve me from trouble; thou shalt compass me about with songs of deliverance. Selah."

—Psalm 32:7

Am I becoming too sensitive? As my years unwind, I'm increasingly teary-eyed when I hear a sentimental song on the radio, and since I listen mostly while driving, I have to be careful when those special songs penetrate my minivan. I could miss my exit or something worse.

In the days when AM radio was king and the Jefferson Starship was an airplane, music seldom made me misty-eyed. It was difficult getting gushy over tunes like "Mony Mony," "Wild Thing," or "Pink Cadillac."

Nowadays, I bawl like a baby when I hear "Butterfly Kisses," "Shout to the Lord," and "I Can Only Imagine." That I choke up <u>every single time</u> I hear each song, no matter how many times I've heard it before, is amazing. Those songs pluck at my heartstrings, and I feel God's tugging through my spiritual speakers.

Do you know what's even more amazing? It's how much God loves me. He loved me long ago with the transistor radio stuck to my ear, and He loves me today. Special songs remind me of His incredible love every time I hear them.

So if you see a guy pulled off the side of the road somewhere with a tissue to his eyes, please don't honk or call for a tow truck. It might just be me listening to a love song from God.

Father, please guard my ears and guide me. Allow me to find You in the songs I listen to.

Refuge and Stronghold

By Bonnie Greenwood Grant

Bible Reading: Psalm 18:1-50

"*As for* God, His way *is* perfect: the word of the Lord is tried: he is a buckler to all those that trust in him."

—Psalm 18:30

My husband took our son, daughter-in-law, and three of my son's friends onto the lake to ride on tubes pulled behind a power boat. Two of the friends climbed onto the tubes, and off they went at high speed, laughing in the spray. My husband realized, after they almost capsized, that they had forgotten to put on their life jackets.

Visions of tragedies filled his mind, as he circled around to pick them up. They could have hit their heads and been knocked out; they could have damaged an arm or leg and not been able to swim; or they could have gotten a cramp and sunk beneath the water. He realized that if any of those things had happened, he might not have been able to find them.

He did find them and got them safely back on board. But that night, he tossed and turned thinking about what could have happened. He tortured himself for not making sure they had on their life jackets. He wondered if he could have lived with the guilt or forgiven himself if something tragic had happened.

Sometimes we forget God's there in the boat with us, and that we don't have to do everything ourselves. He is our buckler and our protector. I wonder how many times a day He protects us from our carelessness.

You are my refuge, O Lord. Surround me and my family with Your angels to protect us. When you act, make it obvious to us that it isn't coincidence, but You at work. Our help comes from You.

Plant Deep Roots

By Charlene Elder

Bible Reading: Mark 4:13-20

"And these are they likewise which are sown on stony ground; who, when they have heard the word, immediately receive it with gladness; And have no root in themselves, and so endure but for a time:…are they which are sown among thorns…and the cares of the world…choke the word, and it becometh unfruitful."

—Mark 4:16-19

It's too easy to assume that once you're a Christian you'll automatically grow spiritually and become a strong believer. Just as soil needs proper preparation in order for plants to grow, your heart needs a continual feeding of God's Word to enable you to grow strong enough to counter the storms of life.

I remember being excited as a child to have my "own" garden in our backyard, though I wasn't real excited about hoeing the ground first and preparing the soil. I just wanted to dig a hole and put my seeds in it; but I prepared the dirt as best as I could, then planted the seeds and watered them daily.

It seemed like forever before I saw several little sprouts breaking through the ground. Within another week, quite a few more had appeared. My garden was growing. But then heavy rains pelted my fledgling plants, and I was devastated. A few days passed, and I noticed that some of my plants were dying—their roots hadn't been strong enough or deep enough to counter the rain that had hammered them. The plants that didn't die grew strong, and I enjoyed their beauty each day.

Today, Lord, I'm reminded not to let rough times in life defeat me or steal Your Word from my heart. Lord, help me plant Your Word deep in my heart so I can stand strong against the storms of life.

Good Enough — Just Not Perfect

By June Parks

Bible Reading: Mark 9:33-37

"Whosoever shall receive one of such children in my name, receiveth me."

—Mark 9:37a

Awhile back, I discovered that I didn't have to be perfect. My house long ago descended from the perfect mark. Dust didn't stand a chance—there were too many papers and objects prohibiting it from settling—but I could never get *everything* just right. I could clean my kitchen until way past bedtime, and still I had to leave something undone. It was never perfect; just clean enough to meet government standards.

Then there were my children. Their words and actions often left something to be desired, so not expecting *perfect* children was definitely a benefit to life. They were better, happier kids when I turned my back on the mess, took cookies outside, and sat on the front steps eating cookies with them and their friends.

They liked for me to play games with them too. They got a good laugh when they saw how slow I had become at trying to run for a base in a pick-up ball game. (Back then, we used a pine tree as first base and an old oak as second. Our black lab insisted on being the hind catcher.)

While the boys played ball, the girls played badminton on the other side of our driveway. Every neighborhood kid got to play something. One Sunday afternoon we made ice cream; everyone came to share the delicious refreshments.

Those memories are dear to me, and I'll bet if you asked my nearly perfect kids, they were great memories for them too.

Thank You, Lord, for the privilege of impacting the lives of children. Draw children everywhere to You and keep them in the warmth of Your smile.

What Stands in Our Way?

By Bill Larmore

Bible Reading: Matthew 19:21-22

"But when the young man heard that saying, he went away sorrowful: for he had great possessions."

—Matthew 19:22

This is the story of a wealthy young man who came to Jesus and the disciples. After hearing Jesus speak, his heart was touched. In fact, he felt led to join the Master. Jesus was drawn to him, but tested his sincerity. The young man passed the interview.

Mark tells us that Jesus loved the man; but then the man asked Jesus a question: "What do I still lack?" Jesus, seeing into his heart, answered him, "… go and sell that thou hast, and give to the poor, and thou shalt have treasure in heaven: and come and follow me." Sorrowfully, the man turned away.

Of course, that must mean that anyone who has great possessions hosts great evil; therefore, those who have riches are irrevocably damned. Why Christ himself, as he later discussed the loss of the young would-be disciple, said, "It is easier for a camel to go through the eye of a needle, than for a rich man to enter the kingdom of God." So… we must be poor to be holy. Right? Wrong.

Each of us has our own personal crutch—tangible or intangible—that if allowed free reign would stand between us and God. Can we afford to keep it? The rich young ruler's barrier was his wealth, which was more important to him than discipleship to Jesus, the holy Son of God.

Jesus waits for us to join Him. What stands in our way?

Dear Jesus, please give me the faith and strength to follow You in discipleship, leaving behind all worldly treasures that were once so dear.

Our Word is Our Bond

By Bonnie Greenwood Grant

Bible Reading: Numbers 30:1-16

"If a man vow a vow unto the Lord, or swear an oath to bind his soul with a bond; he shall not break his word, he shall do according to all that proceedeth out of his mouth."

—Numbers 30:2

Once, a handshake made a binding contract. A person was honor-bound to keep the promise—one's word was his or her bond. Now, it runs more along these lines, "Well, you should have read the fine print," or "You should have gotten it in writing."

My aunt came to Georgia to live with us. She is seventy-seven and lives on Social Security, so she had to get a loan to pay for the moving company to move her. When she was signing the contract, she was forced to pay an additional 10%. After her things were loaded on the truck and half way to Georgia, she got a call saying her goods weighed a thousand pounds more than the estimate, and she owed another $1,000.

When I called and protested, the representative kept saying, "It's a non-binding estimate, and your aunt signed it." In other words, the moving company could give a low quote to get the bid, and then they could charge whatever they wanted.

In their eyes, they thought they had a loophole to fleece their customers. However, God has another system in place to protect His children. We have already been given suggestions for getting around the extra charge. Next I plan to go for the 10% my aunt had to pay.

Lord, help me be a godly person—a person of honor. Let me not give my word lightly. Give me strength to keep my word.

SCALDING TO BALDING

By M.L. Anderson

Bible Reading: Leviticus 13:40-44

"And the man whose hair is fallen off his head, he is bald; *yet* is he clean."

—Leviticus 13:40

At age nine, I embarked on a new hygienic journey: the shower. My dad imposed a rule about hot water. There could be no steam on the bathroom mirror at my shower's end, or I would be in big trouble. I couldn't allow even a trace of a foggy substance anywhere.

Jubilation erupted when I started high school and was able to shower with really hot water after P.E. classes. My naked modesty yielded to the freedom of showering with the faucets set to near scalding temperatures. I would bow my head just below the showerhead and feel the tremendous rush of water clamoring down my head, muffling my ears.

I recall a fellow student telling me I would go bald if I allowed hot water to gush all over my skull. I didn't believe him. Nothing I had learned at that point in school supported such a theory, thus I continued through my high school years to take steamy hot showers at every opportunity. I never showered at home again.

Remember the kid who predicted my future? He was right. I went bald; right in the spot where the water first collided with my old knickerknocker. What a prophecy!

God knows every hair on my head. Too bad He has fewer to know these days. My advice to young men everywhere is this: Take cold showers. Don't steam up the mirror. Save your hair.

Create in me a clean spirit, Lord, and allow me to be grateful even when You take things away.

Possessing the Land

By Charlene Elder

Bible Reading: Joshua 13:1-33

"Now Joshua was old *and* stricken in years; and the Lord said unto him, Thou art old *and* stricken in years, and there remaineth yet very much land to be possessed."

—Joshua 13:1

Have you ever felt that time is slipping by faster than you want? Are there still things you want to do and plans you want to fulfill? The older you get, the more you contemplate what you have accomplished in your life and what you still want to do. Perhaps some of your plans from years ago have been put on the back burner. Are there things in your life that you still want to accomplish?

The Lord called Joshua as a young man to help Moses deliver the Israelites from Egypt and to take them into the Promised Land. Yet by the time Joshua was advanced in years, he and the people had not possessed all that God had planned for them—there was much land yet to be possessed.

What has the Lord provided that you haven't yet possessed? Do you desire a greater, deeper faith, or spiritual gifts, or healing for your physical body? The Lord can fulfill the plans He has for you and give you *the land* (unclaimed blessings and gifts). You can take possession of all that is available for you through Jesus Christ as you dig into God's Word, feed your faith, and walk in faith. The adventure awaits—move forward.

Lord, help my faith grow as I study Your Word, so I can understand and receive all that You have for me.

Disguised Manna

By Susan M. Watkins

Bible Reading: Numbers 14:7-9

"Only rebel not ye against the Lord, neither fear ye the people of the land; for they *are* bread for us: their defense is departed from them, and the Lord is with us: fear them not."

—Numbers 14:9

Positioned for performance—a forty-day recognizance mission provided the answers Moses needed to prepare for possession. The twelve had returned with eyewitness accounts from their calendar of trial. Illuminated nightly by firelight, a dozen voices sang a different song.

They dined on massive grapes, prepared abundance requiring two hands to carry from the Lord's Table—the table set in their enemies' presence. Gradually the spies' hearts turned. Each day wrought new fears, as they examined their fortified enemy. Not trained in warfare, how could they conquer? Four eyes, however, had different vision, hanging the jury.

The spies' return brought joy followed by contagious fear—a plague that rapidly spread and infected all. What did God think? Didn't He realize their opposition? His answer lay tucked in the hearts of Joshua and Caleb. God had meant it when He had faithfully stated, "Trust Me."

Joshua announced, "They are bread for us." Enemies oddly described as food—nourishment. *Sustained by adversity*—the very vehicle by which we're tested equally nourishes us. We often echo fears in our deserts, but careful examination demands a second look. Will God feed us with the very thing we avoid? A bird's eye view becomes mandatory. The presence of our enemy is evidence that we too are positioned for performance.

Our forefathers rose to the challenge. Trusting in God, only two-and-a-half men entered The Promised Land—Joshua, Caleb, and the bones of Joseph. The rest considered God incapable. Man's knees buckled rather than bent.

Lord, open my heart to receive and embrace clear vision.

HOLY ENOUGH

By Bill Larmore

Bible Reading: Romans 5:6-7

"But God commendeth his love toward us, in that, while we were yet sinners, Christ died for us."

—Romans 5:8

It was almost nine P.M. on a drizzly May Monday evening, and I was on my last church visitation call of the evening. I was tired and close to hoping that no one would be home. I knocked on the door and received no response. I was turning away when the door opened. A bearded, unsmiling man stood in the doorway. He smelled strongly of liquor. "Yeah?" he growled. "Whadda you want?"

I grinned at him, despite his expression, and said, "Jesus and I want You. Your wife visited my church last Sunday. I want you to come with her next time."

I expected him to slam the door in my face. Instead, he said, "When I get myself "holy enough" to be inside God's church, I'll be there. I promise." Then he invited me in.

As I shared the Bible with him, he learned that by himself he truly was rotten inside and out. Only Jesus coming into his heart as Savior could make him clean, as clean as Christ had already made me.

God sent Jesus to die for a whiskery drunk, as well as for me, because we could never live holy enough on our own to knock on Heaven's gates. Because of who He is—the Son of God—Jesus loved me *and* the man with the bad breath who wanted to be "holy enough." Jesus extended His open arms of welcome and love to us, even at our worst. Hallelujah!

Dear Lord, please help me carry Your witness with me at all times and in all places because people who need a Savior are everywhere.

STRANGE CAN BE GOOD

By Bonnie Greenwood Grant

Bible Reading: Psalm 9:9-11

"And they that know thy name will put their trust in thee: for thou, Lord, hast not forsaken them that seek thee."

—Psalm 9:10

My granddaughter thinks I'm rather strange. She loves me and knows that I'll be there for her; she knows I want the best for her; but she still thinks I'm strange. I'm strange to her because I pray for help driving out of our subdivision; I pray for help in finding things; and I pray for her protection.

In the past, I have prayed for her to find friends—and she did—and I have prayed for her to have a good day at school—which she had. I pray for nice weather, and sometimes I pray for rain. When God answers my prayers, which He often does, I thank Him openly.

I have learned that when the answers to my prayers—such as my prayers to lose twenty pounds or to get my novel on the NY best seller list—are delayed, that God has a good reason for the delay. I continue to pray because He does not forsake those who seek Him. Praying about life situations may seem strange to my granddaughter, but it is a way of life for me.

Lord, help me trust in You, cherish Your name, and praise You. Help me remember that if something is important to me, it is important to You because You love me. I give You praise and glory, Almighty Father.

Baggage

By Patty Rocco

*Bible Reading: I Corinthians 13;
Philippians 4; Matthew 6:33*

"But seek ye first the kingdom of God, and his righteousness; and all these things shall be added unto you."

—Matthew 6:33

We were ready…or so I thought. We had spent most of the morning packing our camper for a four-day trip. We had packed food, clothes, drinks, firewood, and chairs: there were not only lists, there were sub-lists. My mind reeled from the bustle that had been necessary to prepare for our vacation. When we were about twenty miles away from home, I sighed as I remembered something I had forgotten to pack.

I considered the amount of material comforts that I had packed and then asked God to supply me with my real need—His presence. I sensed that in my busy preparations, I had crowded the rooms of my heart and had pushed God aside. I felt guilty; but He simply asked me to lighten up and search His Word to find that necessary thing I was missing.

I laughed at God's wisdom, knowing that the thing I had forgotten would never hinder my enjoyment of Him.

Father, thank You for providing the creature comforts I enjoy. Remind me, Lord, when I put these things before You that I will miss all that You have for me. Allow me to see You as my overflowing cup and my joy. May I never forget to take You on vacation.

Refresh and Be Refreshed

By Charlene Elder

Bible Reading: Proverbs 11:23-31

"The liberal soul shall be made fat: and he that watereth shall be watered also himself."

—Proverbs 11:25

This verse is still fresh and clear in my memory 33 years after I first heard it shared in a ministerial course. Each class member was given a scripture and seven days in which to prepare a short sermon to present to the class on their scripture verse. One of my class members shared on that particular verse in Proverbs.

Our world is very selfish in its thinking. It urges people to look after their own interests and to disregard the interests of others. In contrast, as believers we are to think of others first.

How many times during a week do we have the opportunity to refresh or *water* someone else with kind words, a generous deed, or a smile? The scripture in Proverbs says that those who are liberal or generous in refreshing others will themselves be refreshed. Each one of us should manifest Proverbs 11:25 in our daily lives.

If we put this verse into practice from a desire to truly see God bless others through us, it won't be long until we are on the receiving end as others refresh us.

Lord, help me refresh others around me with a smile, an encouraging word, or an encouraging deed. I know that as I refresh others, You will refresh me through the words and deeds of others.

For His Good Pleasure

By Adrienne A. Nelson

Bible Reading: Philippians 2:12-18

"For it is God which worketh in you both to will and to do of *his* good pleasure."

—Philippians 2:13

In April, I hung out the red quilt that had kept me warm through the short, but biting Georgia winter. My fellow Southerners and I have no use for cold weather. It's in our agricultural roots. We simply can't get anything "done" on those short, cold days.

In grateful recognition of spring, I draped the quilt, hot from the wash with steam still rising, over the porch railing to dry. I knew it would soon smell as sweet and fresh as the day itself. I was thankful for spring and glad to be getting something accomplished. I knew when I needed the quilt again, I would gratefully enjoy its warmth.

God is like my quilt; He shields me from bitter times with His love. That's how He teaches me and how He gets things "done" in my life. It is not always spring for me, but when I turn to Him, I experience the warmth of His love again and again. During my bitter times, He is with me, surrounding me with comfort. I feel His love in the tasks I perform, from the least to the most important, and I recognize His need to work through me, whatever the season of my soul.

Thank You, Lord, for the physical comfort You graciously provide. Thank You for spiritual guidance and for hands to do Your work. In recognition of Your blessings, may I always answer Your call.

THE CHRISTMAS TREE SEARCH

By June Parks

Bible Reading: Ephesians 6:1-3

"Honor thy father and mother; which is the first commandment with promise."

—Ephesians 6:2

When our family—Mom, Daddy, Betty, and I—went on a search for our Christmas tree in Georgia, it was usually cold and crisp. Mom preferred a cedar tree, so we always visited a farm about eighteen miles from home that abounded with cedars and other seasonal treasures.

Each year, Betty and I ran from one cone-shaped tree to the next squealing, "This one; this one." When we finally discovered the perfect tree—just the right height and fullness—Daddy sawed it down and loaded it on top of our old '36 Ford.

After the tree was secured, we scoured the woods to find a plant called "sweet shrub." It had distinctive maroon-colored flowers that had a clean, sweet smell when handled. It created a real Christmas memory.

Sticker bushes were another must-have…no leaves, just silver limbs that were loaded with stickers. On our return home, Betty and I would put multi-colored gum drops on each and every sticker. Mom *loved* a gumdrop tree.

On that farm there was a wide, fast-flowing stream bordered by huge flat rocks. An overhanging rock there—the size of a car—had a crack in it. My ingenious Daddy shoved a stick into the crack, put a big pot on it, built a fire under it, and boiled our hot dogs. A rack inside the pot steamed our buns. A squirt of mustard and catsup rendered those "dogs" perfect.

That Christmas tree search each year was our beloved tradition. Our family drew closer because of those wonderful traditions.

Dear Lord, thank You for all my childhood memories. My present days are better because of those past happenings. Thank You for Your blessings.

Take and Eat

By Bonnie Greenwood Grant

Scripture Reading: Genesis 1:1-31

"And God said, Let the earth bring forth grass, the herb yielding seed, *and* the fruit tree yielding fruit after his kind, …and it was so."

—Genesis 1:11

I was looking through my vitamin catalog and happened to glance at the pages of herbs. I was amazed at the number of common plants—cinnamon, turmeric, oregano—that had health benefits. God was obviously not frivolous when He created plants. They all have a purpose.

Equisetum (horsetail), considered to be a weed, has healing properties. Kudzu, another weed that has almost covered the South in crawling green vines, is used to help recovering alcoholics. Who knew?

When I read that the state-of-the-art, top-of-the-line cancer preventer and cure was raw organic carrots, God put it together for me. I knew the expressions, "you are what you eat," and "food is medicine," and I partially understood the concept. This time, a picture of God forming a human out of clay surrounded by the plants that He had made came to my mind. God made plants for us. He designed our molecular structure to mesh with their molecular structure.

How does the diet God designed for us compare with what most people are eating today? Many of today's foods are genetically modified, micro waved, preserved, and fried and are washed down with sugary sodas. In spite of our poor eating habits, God made a provision. Scientists have discovered that one of our vices—dark chocolate—contains antioxidants, polyphenols and Oligomers, which prevent bad cholesterol from building up in our arteries. Now wasn't it nice of God to put good things in chocolate?

Lord, You are wondrous. You made all of creation to work together. Thank You for creating us and making provision for us.

Songs of Deliverance

By Charlene Elder

Bible Reading: Psalm 32:1-11

"Thou *art* my hiding place; thou shalt preserve me from trouble; thou shalt compass me about with songs of deliverance. Selah."

—Psalm 32:7

I remember listening to the testimony of Corrie ten Boom, a survivor of the German occupation of Holland during the 1940's. She and her family were instrumental in helping Jews leave the country through the underground movement. Within their home a normal-looking bookcase became a hiding place for Jews on their journey through the Dutch underground.

In 1944, the ten Boom family was arrested and sent to prison. Corrie was the only one of her family to survive the ordeals of prison and torture. At the end of 1944, she was summoned to the prison headquarters and given her "release" papers. She did not question the officials but took her meager belongings and left. Later, she learned that they had made a mistake, but it was too late by then; the others her age in the prison were all killed shortly after her departure.

After her release, Corrie told the story of how the Lord had become her hiding place when she had been confined to a small prison cell.

You may not have had to face prison, slavery, or the Holocaust, but when you face problems in life, you can experience God's presence and protection as Corrie and others did.

Thank You, Lord, that You are my hiding place today. When troubles surround me on all sides and I am overwhelmed, I will trust in You. You are my refuge and my fortress. Thank You for rescuing me so I can sing of Your deliverance.

His Eye is On the Sparrow

By Diana J. Baker

Bible Reading: Matthew 6:25-34

"Behold the fowls of the air: for they sow not, neither do they reap, nor gather into barns; yet your heavenly Father feedeth them. Are ye not much better than they?"

—Matthew 6:26

I heard the sparrows, cardinals, and chickadees singing as I fought the wind to fill the brightly colored feeders in my yard. I knew the birds were not concerned about the wind, the rain that would soon follow, or where they would find their next meal. When God created them, He programmed them to trust Him for their provision. They never worried; they just kept singing and praising God, knowing He would meet their needs.

I realized that I often fretted and worried about finances, family situations, and myriads of other things. It wasn't that I didn't have faith in God; it was just that at times I leaned on my own understanding and abilities to solve problems rather than leaning on God's ability.

When I finished filling the feeders, I returned to the house and sat down in my favorite chair in front of the bay window. Within minutes, the birds were happily darting back and forth singing and munching on seeds. I prayed, making a fresh commitment to rest my needs in God's hands, to praise and worship Him daily, and to glorify Him with my life.

Thank You, Lord, for the wonderful ways You have provided for me. Please help me have faith in Your provision today, knowing that if You take care of the tiniest sparrow, You will surely take care of me. Help me encourage others to look to You for Your provision for them.

To Catch a Fly—
Honey vs. Vinegar

By Bonnie Greenwood Grant

Scripture Focus: Ephesians 4:29-32

"Let no corrupt communication proceed out of your mouth, but that which is good to the use of edifying, that it may minister grace unto the hearers."

—Ephesians 4:29

When my husband was young, his mother flew into a rage whenever she saw his report card. He got A's in academic subjects, but got a C—or worse—in conduct. "Why can't you get all A's like your big brother?" she questioned. Consequently, Kerry gave up trying to please her. During his senior year in high school, he even tried his best to flunk out.

My father, in contrast, focused on good things. "Did you write that? That's really good," he would say. Even when I was a child, he asked my opinion and valued it.

When my father read about a study involving three high school track coaches and three methods of coaching, it reinforced his approach to life. One coach criticized the athletes for what they did wrong. One praised them for what they did right. The last coach did both. The 'praised' group improved more than the others, proving the old adage that you can catch more flies with honey than with vinegar.

The apostle Paul knew that it was human nature to find fault, and he warned against it because it caused discord. Critical people were no fun to be around. Christians were supposed to be rejoicing because they were filled with the Holy Spirit and were in tune with their Creator. Paul admonished Christians to 'think on the good things that would build each other up.'

Lord, help me focus on the beauty of the people around me and not on their faults. Help me see people through Your eyes.

Faithful Until the End

By Judy Becker

Bible Reading: Luke 2:25-38

"The righteous shall flourish like the palm tree: he shall grow like a cedar in Lebanon. Those that be planted in the house of the Lord shall flourish… They shall still bring forth fruit in old age; they shall be fat and flourishing."

—Psalm 92:12-14

Simeon and Anna had shown a constancy of service when they met Mary and Joseph at Jesus' temple dedication. Both were well up in years; both were still serving the Lord with fervency.

The Holy Spirit had revealed to Simeon that he would see Christ before he died, and the Spirit led him to the temple at the very moment when Mary and Joseph were there. It was no accident that Anna came in at the same time. They had both been looking for the Messiah and had been fellowshipping with others who were watching. Simeon left the temple that day rejoicing in the Lord's fulfilled word. Anna went out to spread the word that Christ had come.

The Church today also has its gray-headed servers. Seeing believers faithfully serving into old age is a beautiful thing. Many are widowed, like Anna, and are free to serve the Lord completely. Some are in a ministry of proclaiming His coming again—they are watchers like Anna and Simeon. They realize the signs of the times because they know much of the Word.

When I go to conferences, I see vigorous older men—healthy and flourishing like a palm tree—standing at the pulpit. Even the audiences are heavily sprinkled with the gray-haired of both sexes. It seems that the longer we walk with the Lord, the more we long to see His Word fulfilled.

Lord, please help me continue to faithfully serve You unto the end.

Watch Your Language

By Charlene Elder

Bible Reading: Proverbs 18:15-21

"Life and death are in the power of the tongue..."

—Proverbs 18:21

The Word says that life *and* death are in the power of our tongues. The responsibility of how we speak is up to us. Will we speak life, or will we speak death?

If we have children, we know how easy it is for them to let "words" slip out of their mouths—especially words they've heard at school or play. Instructing them in wholesome speech and then disciplining them when improper words are spoken goes without saying; but as parents, we need to "practice what we preach." It's too easy to remind our children that "we don't talk like that" and five minutes later use some of the same language because we're upset.

The Lord makes it plain in His Word that we have the ability to speak life or death through the words we choose. "I'm dying to see that movie" may not be what we really mean…are we really *dying* to go see a movie? What about, "I'll probably get the flu again this year—like I do every year." Did I just set myself up again for failure?

Proverbs says that a perverted mouth is a disobedient mouth. It may be time for us to line up our speech with God's Word and to speak LIFE.

Lord, help me speak life-giving words from Your Word and not negative or empty words.

Teamwork

By Bonnie Greenwood Grant

Bible Reading: Matthew 11: 28-30

"For my yoke is easy, and my burden is light."

—Matthew 11:30

Recently, God showed me the truth of this verse. I went to lunch with my husband, and I set my purse on the table to get the camera lens cover out for my husband to fix. We returned home after lunch, and as I climbed out of the car, my neighbor asked if I would check my yard for a large inflatable Easter egg that had escaped. I promised to search and to return the egg if I found it.

I walked down my steep side yard, looking for the egg and pulling weeds as I searched. I didn't find the egg, so I went back up the hill. Later, I needed something in my purse and panicked when I couldn't find my purse anywhere. I searched everywhere. The restaurant did cross my mind, but I didn't think I left my purse there, because it had sat beside my plate the whole time I was there. Surely I would have picked it up when I finished lunch.

I thought I might have left the purse outside when I pulled weeds. I ran down the hill, but didn't find it. *Where could it be?* I wondered. *I've wasted 25 minutes racing around trying to do it my way. I'm just going to pray about it.*

"Lord, where is my purse?"

"Call the restaurant," I heard in my spirit.

I called the restaurant. "Yes, your purse is here," the waitress said. "It was sitting right on the table in plain sight, so I put it behind the counter to keep it safe."

Lord, thank You for protecting my belongings. Please help me pray first when a problem arises. Life is so much easier when I do.

A Gentle Man

By Darlene Applegate

Bible Reading: I Corinthians 13:1-7

"Charity suffereth long, *and* is kind; charity envieth not; charity vaunteth not itself, is not puffed up."

—I Corinthians 13:4

When I read I Corinthians 13:4, I think of my husband, David. He is gentle, kind, and patient. He is not jealous, never brags, and is not arrogant. My husband's walk exemplifies what God characterizes as love. David loves me the way Christ loves the church.

Of course, that doesn't mean I get everything I want or demand. When necessary, David is quite capable of being stern. Occasionally, my pouting does get me what I want, but afterwards I don't enjoy it like I thought I would. Over time, I have learned that listening and following my husband's guidance does bring blessings and protections to my life—blessings and protections given by God and delivered through my husband.

It's hard to admit, but true, that sometimes my advice is not what my husband wants to hear. Still, he carefully weighs my thoughts because he understands that he answers to God for his decisions. He takes that responsibility seriously.

I hope my love for David is representative of the Spirit of God who lives within me. I desire to become a *Proverbs 31 woman* who honors her husband in all things. The scriptures clearly tell us that faith, hope, and love abide, but the greatest of the three is love.

Father, bless my family with an abundance of patience, kindness, meekness, humility, and love. Bless the works of our hands. When people enter our home, may they find it full of love, joy, peace, and happiness.

Unseen Answers

By Susan M. Watkins

Bible Reading: Luke 1:41-45

"And blessed *is* she that believed: for there shall be a performance of those things which were told her from the Lord."

—Luke 1:45

Fifteen years old. Bible scholars agree that was Mary's age when Gabriel knocked on the door of her tender life. Staring into the impossible, she asks the question humanity asks when natural encounters supernatural: "How can this be?"

Gabriel removes the intellectual barriers and explains God's unrestricted plan. Mary believes the unbelievable, and the most important seed ever planted in the earth is placed in the womb of this young Jewish virgin.

Has God promised you something that makes you ask Mary's question? Waiting for the performance, or fulfillment, is an arduous task. Faith stretches to the point of tearing. God understands. When He told Abraham he would become a one-hundred-year-old father, time crawled before Isaac did. God knew Abraham would struggle waiting to send the birth announcements. That's why He equipped him with the promise. When his hope was deferred, he was able to unfold God's statement kept passionately tucked inside his pocket of faith.

God punctuates His reliability in Genesis one. In a six-day period, every statement, "And God said," is followed with the underscored proclamation, "and it was so." Thus God announced to every human being—it is safe to trust Him.

Two things are activated when we believe beyond our human reasoning. We're first blessed, as described in the above verse, and then it is reckoned unto us as righteousness. God is motivated and moved by our faith in Him. If He's called you to believe Him for something seemingly impossible, disregard the naysayer and focus solely on His faithfulness. The unseen is the only accurate depiction of reality.

Father, with You as my Shepherd, I can relax.

Standing in Faith

By Patty Rocco

Bible Reading: Romans 4

"For what saith the scripture? Abraham believed God, and it was counted unto him for righteousness."

—Romans 4:3

It was supposed to be a simple procedure—a surgery to fix a botched surgery. Although the surgery had gone well the second time around, someone had forgotten about the possibility of a blood clot. Now a family met in an ICU waiting room to determine what hope they could cling to. The doctor's report had been bad. It was mom's birthday and a bitter shock.

A prayer warrior encouraged me to think about Abraham. Abraham never wavered in unbelief, but instead held fast to God's promise. He saw things that were not as though they had already happened. He believed even when everyone else around him did not. Like Abraham, we had to choose, and we had to pray. God encouraged us to hold on to our small thread of hope.

Hope doesn't disappoint. As the hours yawned by, reports of small improvement trickled in. Mom's color changed; her blood pressure rose; she moved her arms and fluttered her eyelids. We are amazed at God's faithfulness and how He answered our prayers.

Father, I am amazed at Your graciousness. I thank You for answering my prayers for big things and for small. Help me walk as Abraham walked, never wavering in unbelief.

A Mother's Concern

By Brenda Thompson Ward

Bible Reading: Psalm 3:1-4

"My voice shalt thou hear in the morning, O Lord; in the morning will I direct *my prayer* unto thee, and will look up."

—Psalm 5:3

It's now 2:00 A.M., and I'm <u>wide awake</u>. I know the Lord is awakening me to pray for one of my children. When He wakes me at this hour of the morning, I know it's for a reason.

When I went to bed last night, I had been burdened about a problem one of my children had talked to me about yesterday. It's not a problem that's new to most of us. We've all been there—when we were young, married, had little children, and the week was longer than the paycheck.

My first reaction to the situation, I'm ashamed to say, had been to mull over how I could help fix the problem. That's why I'm awake at two in the morning. I now realize I cannot take care of my adult children's problems. My first response should have been to take the problem to the feet of Jesus and turn it over to Him. Had I done that, I'd probably be asleep right now.

Sometimes, I forget that all I have to do is ask in faith, trust with my whole heart, and wait on the Lord to answer. However, I know that as I wait on the Lord and encourage my child to wait on Him, He will meet all of our needs according to His riches in Christ Jesus.

Dear Lord, thank You for Your ever watchful eye. Help me to remember that I need to turn to You first and not depend on myself.

Trust

By Bonnie Greenwood Grant

Bible Reading: Romans 12: 9-15

"Rejoicing in hope; patient in tribulation; continuing instant in prayer."
—Romans 12:12

Clouds were gathering and the wind was whipping the lake into choppy waves. My son-in-law put the finishing touches on his famous grilled chicken as I walked to the lake to call everyone to dinner. My husband was in his canoe pushing himself away from the seawall and out into the lake with his paddle.

"Honey, dinner is ready," I called.
"I want to fish for awhile; I'll be up shortly," he replied.
"Honey, the weather is getting bad. Why don't you come and eat?"
"I waited 15 years to get this canoe into the water, and I feel like fishing."
During dinner my family and I noted the weather worsening.
"Dad didn't have his life jacket on did he?" my daughter asked.
We prayed for his safety.
After dinner, I heard the shower. My husband was back.
"What happened?" I asked after his shower.
"My canoe capsized. I've never been so scared in my life; but I remembered from Boy Scout drills—when your canoe capsizes, don't panic. My clothes made it difficult to swim, and the canoe was underwater, but I didn't want to let it sink because I knew I'd never find it. I was in the water about 45 minutes. It was freezing. I towed the canoe to a dock and was able to get out of the water only because the dock had a ladder attached."

I smiled. *God had known my husband would do something stupid when he was sixty-five, and He had made provision for his safety fifty-five years ahead of time.*

Lord, help me trust You in all circumstances, knowing You have already prepared the way through my difficulties.

Perfect Peace

By Judy Parrott

Bible Reading: John 14:11-21

"Thou wilt keep him in perfect peace, whose mind is stayed on *thee*: because he trusteth in thee."

—Isaiah 26:3

My husband takes a blood thinner to protect his mechanical heart valve from clots. This powerful drug sometimes accumulates and brings on a frightening blood loss. He turns pale or passes out, and we are off to the hospital for another transfusion.

I have heard that God trains us to trust Him with a promise, a problem, and a provision. One day, I found Jeremiah 29:11: "For I know the thoughts that I think toward you, saith the Lord, thoughts of peace, and not of evil, to give you an expected end."

The next day my husband had to go to the hospital again, and that promise encased me with a wonderful peace. He was given two pints of blood, but doctors suspected surgery was needed to stop the bleeding. As I prayed for him, the Lord spoke to my heart, "Fear not." When the doctor inspected my husband's intestines, he found only slight inflammation and surgery was not needed.

We received our provision. Jesus said He gives us peace, not as the world gives. It is a precious fruit of His Spirit that we can't live without if we want to stay in good health.

Dear Lord, I am grateful that You always bring me peace when I give You my burdens. Thank You for Your trustworthy promises in times of trouble.

What Do You Have in Your Hand?

By Diana J. Baker

Bible Reading: Exodus 4:1-5; Exodus 14:16, 21-31

"And the Lord said unto him, what *is* that in thine hand? And he said, A rod."
—Exodus 4:2

God is a deliverer. His purpose has always been to deliver man from the bondage of sin, to bring him into right relationship with Himself, and to equip him to bring deliverance to others. The Bible is filled with deliverers. They used the things that God had placed in their hands to set captives free.

God spoke to Moses from the burning bush and asked him what he had in his hand. God used the rod in Moses' hand to release His people from the hand of Pharaoh.

God equipped David, the shepherd boy, with a slingshot and 5 smooth stones—not exactly the weaponry we'd desire if we faced a giant. However, because God had proven His faithfulness to David through his defeat of a lion and a bear, David trusted Him to bring victory through what was in his hand—his slingshot—and what was in his heart—faith in the power of God.

God has placed gifts, talents, and abilities in our hands to use to fight the good fight of faith. We may not have a rod or a slingshot, but we do have the Word of God, salvation through faith in the Lord Jesus Christ, the power of the Holy Spirit, and natural and spiritual gifts. We, like Moses and David, need to take what is in our hand and use it for the glory of God.

What do you have in your hand?

Father, help me grow in faith and in the knowledge of You and Your Word. Help me use my gifts and talents to deliver others.

An Anchor That Holds

By Jack G. Elder

Bible Reading: Hebrews 6:18-20

"Which *hope* we have as an anchor of the soul, both sure and stedfast, and which entereth into that within the veil."

—Hebrews 6:19

We live in a fast-changing society in the computer age. In fact, we can hardly get a new computer home before it's obsolete. Old institutions we thought would always exist are disappearing. The work place is changing on a daily basis. *Life* magazine is gone! Even the weather seems to be changing. There is not a lot to hang our hats on anymore. Nothing in this world generates hope. Nothing anchors drifting lives.

Yet, we have a hope that anchors our souls. An anchor holds a ship in place regardless of the wind and waves. It digs into the bottom of the sea and keeps the ship steady. There are many anchor designs, but they all must hold. Regardless of the design, an anchor must keep a vessel from drifting.

Fear not, fellow sea voyagers, there is an anchor that holds. Our hope in Jesus is a sure and steadfast anchor in this turbulent age. We have an unshakable anchor that will not change ever.

It is comforting to know that no matter what goes on around us, no matter how the politics change, or even how the weather changes, there is a hope that never changes. We have an anchor in life holding us steady through all the chaotic changes in the world.

Thank You, Father, for Your Son Jesus, who is my anchor. He keeps me steady in all the storms and turbulence I face every day.

A Tired Christian

By Brenda Thompson Ward

Bible Reading: Isaiah 40:28-31

"Hast thou not known? hast thou not heard, *that* the everlasting God, the Lord, the Creator of the ends of the earth, fainteth not, neither is weary? *there* is no searching of his understanding."

—Isaiah 40:28

This morning, I'm exhausted from lack of sleep for the last two nights. The air conditioner upstairs is on the blink, but is supposed to be repaired today. In desperation, I attempted to sleep downstairs last night, but all I did was toss, turn, and think.

Around 4:30 A.M., I finally gave up on sleep and got up. However, I had no energy to do the things I needed to do. In that state of mind, I opened my Bible and the verse above immediately caught my eye.

I was reminded that God is well aware of my condition. When I think about how many people there are in the world and how great their needs are, I am astonished to know that God is never weary and does not ever get tired.

I know that God will help me make it through my duties of the day. Perhaps then I can return to my home and fall onto the love seat (short people fit well on a love seat) for a much-needed nap.

What a great comfort it is to know how untiring God is. He is never too busy, and He will never tell us to make an appointment to see Him. He is always alert and available to His children.

Lord, help me keep in mind that You can provide all the strength I need to have a good day. Help me to never be too tired to spend daily time with You.

In Times of Trouble: Rejoice!

By Judy Becker

Bible Reading: Habakkuk 1:1-4, 13; Habakkuk 2:1-3

"Although the fig tree shall not blossom, neither *shall* fruit be in the vines; the labour of the olive shall fail, and the fields shall yield no meat; the flock shall be cut off from the fold, and *there shall* be no herd in the stalls: Yet I will rejoice in the Lord, I will joy in the God of my salvation."

—Habakkuk 3:17-18

We often hear that "the world is going to hell in a hand basket." Habakkuk must have decided the same thing. He lamented about the evil in the world and cried out to God, "Don't you care, O God, that the wicked seem to have the upper-hand? How can You who are holy look on such as deal treacherously?"

Had God lost control? No. He was being longsuffering, not willing that any should perish. His mercy does have a limit, however, as He showed Habakkuk. God gave him a vision of what was coming. It was not coming immediately, but it was a sure vision. God told him the vision would not tarry. In other words, it would come on time. Habakkuk was willing to go through the hard times just to see justice done.

We know the wicked of our day will answer to God's justice too. Therefore, we can rejoice with Habakkuk in spite of how bad things look. God is still reigning, and wickedness will have an end in His own good time. So Christian, rejoice! If you read the end of The Book, you will see that Christ and His Church win.

O Lord, let me rejoice in Your Word and remain faithful in the difficult times, knowing all things rest firmly under Your control.

The Prize

By Louise Flanders

*Bible Reading: Luke 9:62; I Corinthians 9:24;
Hebrews 12:1-2; Philippians 2:16*

"Know ye not that they which run in a race run all, but one receiveth the prize? So run, that ye may obtain."

—I Corinthians 9:24

"Hurry! Run faster. Keep going and don't look back." The bleachers were packed with enthusiastic fans waving banners and shouting words of encouragement to their special athletes.

Our son, Jonathan, loved to run, so we decided to enroll him in a Special Olympics relay race. He trained diligently for the race, and we could hardly wait for the big event.

The day of the race dawned sunny and warm. Excitement filled the air. When Jonathan's turn came, he ran with abandonment, leaving the other athletes behind. He won the first of many gold medals that day.

In order to win the race and gain the coveted prize, an athlete must be willing to discipline himself and must often forego what is good or better in order to obtain the best. He must exercise patience as he trains his body, mind, and spirit for the challenge ahead.

The Christian life is a race that can be won successfully, if we are willing to discipline ourselves to spend time daily in God's Word and to make prayer a priority in our daily routine. Spiritual growth, like physical growth, is often a slow process that requires patience and consistency. If we seek God's perfect will for our lives, we can successfully run the race that He has set before us.

Father, help me be consistent in my daily walk with You. Help me discipline my time, my talents, and my resources to be used for Your purpose and Your glory.

Fruit in the Wilderness

By Judy Parrott

Bible Reading: II Corinthians 4

"Persecuted, but not forsaken; cast down, but not destroyed; Always bearing about in the body the dying of the Lord Jesus, that the life also of Jesus might be made manifest in our body."

—II Corinthians 4:9-10

Alicia fled for her life from Mexico to Texas after her Christian orphanage was confiscated by the government. In Texas, she was given a tiny trailer without power or water. The stench of garbage in the trailer park nauseated her, criminals dominated the park, and gunshots alarmed her every night. It was so dangerous the police avoided the place.

Alicia became depressed. "Lord, what have I done to deserve such chastening?" she prayed.

God answered, "I came down from a holy place to a similar trash dump two thousand years ago and stayed for 33 years. I love you. You have never said "no" to Me."

Alicia wept with relief. Her self-pity dissolved. Communication with God was restored, and she boldly asked Him if He would mind removing the trash.

One day, a garbage truck stopped in front of her trailer. The truck driver, a Christian, said he had orders to come, although he had never been there before. He hauled out garbage without charge for three weeks until the park was clean.

Alicia shined light where God had planted her, and He answered her prayers. She passed His love on, while working daily to beautify her tiny yard. Gradually, the neighbors followed suit, and respectability bloomed.

Dear Lord, You are wonderful to meet my needs through Jesus. You aren't angry with me. You always answer me. I give You my sacrifice of praise. Help me bloom where I am planted, knowing You will provide the increase.

God's Candle

By Susan M. Schulz

Bible Reading: Romans 8:28-39

"The spirit of man *is* the candle of the Lord, searching all the inward parts of the belly."

—Proverbs 20:27

To remain ready for God's candle to search our inmost parts can be a challenge. Our part requires a willingness to look with God to see what holds us back from a vibrant, on-fire relationship with Him. God tried repeatedly to get me to cooperate with Him, but my refusal to dig up my anger and hurt over my brother's murder hindered the process. During the grieving process, I buried anger towards God deep in the caverns of my heart. As a result, I ignored God for years.

Things changed at the birth of my first child. My spiritual life began to be restored, but something was holding me back; a problem remained. I had not dealt with my issues.

God never gave up on me. He was like a miner digging for gold—lighted helmet and all. He led me as I prayed, completed Bible studies, read books, and attended conferences. His lamp shown brighter and brighter into the eyes of my heart until I finally saw the misdirected resentment I had toward Him for allowing my brother to be taken away in the prime of his life.

When God revealed my anger, it melted in His hands. Now, when I am tempted to bury my frustrations, I look where His light shines, confess, and move on with Him.

Dear Lord, keep Your light shining. Search me and know my anxious thoughts. Thank You for Your healing and forgiveness. Lead me in the way everlasting. I love You with all of my heart, soul, mind, and strength.

Not Being Rich Toward God

By Marcus Beavers

Bible Reading: Luke 12:13-21

"So is he that layeth up treasure for himself, and is not rich toward God."
—Luke 12:21

Jesus, the Son of God, never said that being in need was a virtue. Instead, He made it clear that the love of riches was shortsighted and lead to personal ruin for those who trusted only in material wealth.

Christ was asked to help with an inheritance squabble between brothers. He did not sympathize with the questioner's motives; instead He warned against coveting. There is a *richness* that is important, and Christ wants every person to know that richness.

Many Christians equate prosperity with God's material blessings. Perhaps the man in Jesus' parable thought that. The landowner had a great harvest and rebuilt huge barns to store it all in. He was set to enjoy life, thinking he could depend on his wealth as lasting security.

The final reality is that the infinite personal God exists, and to know and obey Him is richness. Human choices are significant, and men do amazing things. But we are commanded to love and obey God as our main purpose and for our lasting good.

Jesus emphasized in His parable the results of truth and error. If we ignore God and His commands, our end will be terrible. Jesus told how God called the rich man a fool. The rich farmer worked hard and set up his good retirement, but was not prepared for God's judgment and his resulting poverty before Him.

Most Holy God, Creator, Sustainer, and Disposer of all things, I want to know and understand You better. You are good and merciful to all. I want to be rich toward You.

Twenty-Twenty Vision

By Jack G. Elder

Bible Reading: Proverbs 29:18-23

"Where *there* is no vision, the people perish: but he that keepeth the law, happy is he."

—Proverbs 29:18

I have worn glasses since I was in the third grade. Without glasses, life would be a blur. That's the immediate thought I get from the word *vision*. The Bible often compares spiritual things with physical things. In this passage in Proverbs, the writer compares not keeping the law or the Word to having no vision or being blind. In other words, the Word contains the vision or revelation for our lives. Without knowing our purpose and direction, we wander as those who have no vision.

The word *perish* includes the idea of losing restraint. We see in the world today those who have lost all restraint and indulge in all manner of evil desires. This verse makes it clear that the way to happiness and blessing is through knowing the Word and getting a clear twenty-twenty vision of life. This is the *only* way to true happiness. This is the path we all must take if we are to receive all the blessings God has in store for us.

The Declaration of Independence affirms that the Creator endowed us with the right to pursue happiness. The Word of God tells us how to catch happiness. Read the Word—keep the Word.

Lord, help me see clearly the path You have for me. Guide me over that path through my careful observance of Your Word.

God Is With Us

By Gail Pallotta

Bible Reading: Psalm 46

"Be still, and know that I *am* God. I will be exalted among the heathen, I will be exalted in the earth."

—Psalm 46:10

Recognizing that God is God is reassuring. The majority of us probably realize this more easily when we are relaxed. It was especially evident to me this past summer while I was on vacation and walked along the beach at night. The lapping of the waves seemed to echo peacefulness. The moon shining on the ocean reflected God's light in the darkness. The sound of the ocean lulled away my worldly cares, while the magnitude of the waters conveyed God's power, and the beauty of the evening declared His glory.

Unfortunately, it is about six hours from my home to the nearest beach. However, I believe I can feel God's presence and comfort wherever I am, if I take the time. I can experience it in the warm sunshine of a bright day. It sparkles in the glittery heavens at night. It bursts forth with fresh spring flowers that gloriously color my world. It kindles my heart with love. It is in the answers to my prayers.

Dear God, thank You for revealing Yourself to me in the world, at church, and in my fellow man. Help me know Your presence and be comforted by it.

THE RICHES OF CHRIST

By Judy Becker

Bible Reading: Isaiah 64:1-4; Ephesians 1:12, 18, 2:7; Malachi 3:17

"But as it is written, Eye hath not seen, nor ear heard, neither have entered into the heart of man, the things which God hath prepared for them that love him."

—I Corinthians 2:9

Think of it, beloved ones of the Lord; we are His riches! We are His inheritance in the saints, and we are the jewels of His treasure. Yet He also has riches indescribable for us. Paul calls them unsearchable riches—ones past finding out. Isaiah tells us that He will literally move mountains to prepare a place for His people, and when He is through, the whole earth will be different. Meanwhile, we shall be with Him in that glorious city. Beloved, do you not rejoice to be so cherished?

In 1981, Marie, one of my best friends died. As another of her good friends stood with me looking down at her body, my friend said, "Drat, she beat us *to the glory.*" Both of us had spent many hours on the phone with Marie talking about the Lord.

On Marie's tombstone they inscribed part of Psalm 16:11, "In thy presence is fullness of joy." The rest of that verse says "in his right hand are pleasures for evermore." I'm sure Marie is enjoying those pleasures to the fullest even now. She was surely one of His precious jewels.

We, too, shall all enter into those pleasures one day when He says to His Bride, "Rise up, my love, my fair one, and come away."

Thank You, Lord, for Your great love for me. Let me never lose the hope of my calling in You or forget to watch for Your appearance. I love You, Lord.

Giving Up Habits

By Judy Parrott

Bible Reading: Romans 6; Romans 7

"But now being made free from sin, and become servants to God, ye have your fruit unto holiness, and the end everlasting life."

—Romans 6:22

My friend, Ella, told me about how she was able to break her habit of smoking three packs of cigarettes a day. She had tried everything. One night she was awakened and heard a voice saying, "You don't need cigarettes any more." She fell back asleep. The next morning about ten o'clock she realized she had not had a cigarette that day, nor had she wanted one. She never wanted another one.

Arlene smoked three packs a day and loved smoking. After she became a Christian, she sensed words in her mind saying, "Do you want to quit?"

"*No! I love my cigarettes,*" she thought.

A second time, very gently, she 'heard' the words in her spirit, "Will you set them down?"

The love in that voice stirred her more than her love for the cigarettes.

"Yes, Lord," she replied.

That very moment she lost her desire for cigarettes and never wanted them again. She feared that she would gain weight, but her fear dissipated when she noticed her weight didn't change. She was surrounded by smokers yet was not tempted. God's love for her was greater than her love for the addiction.

Once these women recognized the voice of God within, they realized a choice had to be made. Their relationship with God became far more important than smoking.

Dear Lord, these experiences give me hope in my own weaknesses. Thank You for helping me with all my infirmities. Nothing is too hard for You.

Casting Shadows or Light

By Brenda Thompson Ward

Bible Reading: II Timothy 1:3-9

"When I call to remembrance the unfeigned faith that is in thee, which dwelt first in thy grandmother Lois, and thy mother Eunice; and I am persuaded that in thee also."

—II Timothy 1:5

I have been told repeatedly that people watch our actions. Being responsible for our actions is a big assignment for Christians. It terrifies me that I might be responsible for someone not coming to the Lord because they saw sin in my life.

Our lives either shed light or cast shadows. Our fast-paced world has taught us to want instant attention—whether in a store, on the phone, or on the Internet. We have become accustomed to quick results and having things our way.

We are the light and salt of the world. We all have pressures and obligations, but we also have something the world desperately needs: The Lord Jesus Christ. Therefore, we should behave in an unselfish manner that reflects Christ. It would be terrible to be in such a hurry that we ignored the signs of someone who is troubled. We must walk in unfeigned faith and Christlikeness as Timothy did.

Lord, help me remain mindful that I am a walking representative for You. Let me not forget that my actions should always reflect Your love.

CHARIOTS OF FIRE

By Charlene Elder

Bible Reading: Hebrews 12:1-3

"Wherefore seeing we also are compassed about with so great a cloud of witnesses, let us lay aside every weight, and the sin which doth so easily beset *us*, and let us run with patience the race that is set before us, Looking unto Jesus the author and finisher of *our* faith; who for the joy that was set before him endured the cross, despising the shame, and is set down at the right hand of the throne of God."

—Hebrews 12:1-2

Do you remember relay races in elementary school and track meets in high school? Maybe you didn't participate in track, but at some point as a child you were probably in a race of some kind, and you wanted to run the fastest and win.

There are many references in God's Word to believers running the race of life with steadfastness and perseverance. A good example was shared with the world in 1981 in the movie, *Chariots of Fire*. It exemplified the perseverance of Eric Liddell, a man who loved to run. Eric was also a devoted Christian and wanted to bring the Lord glory through his running. He trained and practiced, and he persevered with a zealous commitment that parlays all Olympic gold medalists.

Eric Liddell did win, not only as a runner, but as a follower of the Lord. He later became a missionary to China. His great example encourages everyone to persevere with patience and faith in the race that is set before them.

Lord, sometimes I get weary and want to give up; but You promised a life of blessing if I persevere. Thank You for giving me needed strength to "run the race."

Remedy for Guilt

By Cynthia L. Simmons

Bible Reading: Romans 8:1–8

"There *is* therefore now no condemnation to them which are in Christ Jesus, who walk not after the flesh, but after the Spirit."

—Romans 8:1

I'm a perfectionist. If I earned a ninety-six on my final exam, the four points I missed flustered me so much that I couldn't enjoy my success. That attitude still lingers, even though I've been out of school for many years. Sometimes I even fume that I don't get grades anymore. At least grades made me feel I earned the teacher's praise.

Now I often feel like I don't measure up. The memory of a forgotten chore, a foolish statement, a sin from the past, or a selfish action can set my heart ablaze with fresh guilt.

One morning during my devotions, I listed my sins and failures before the Lord. As I recalled each incident, guilt seared my heart. "Lord, how can You stand me? I wouldn't blame You if You despised me," I prayed.

Suddenly, an image flashed into my mind. I sat in a chair, and the Savior stood beside me. He had His hand on my shoulder, and I could feel the glow of His love. Even though I wasn't perfect and even hated my own sin, He didn't condemn me, because He had paid for my sin. My guilt disappeared, and I felt His acceptance and love. What a miracle!

"Lord, the guilt of sin often torments my mind. Remind me that You paid for my sins, and I'm not condemned. Speak Your peace to my soul. Thank You for loving me so much."

The Narrow Gate

By Judy Parrott

Bible Reading: Luke 13:23-30

"Strive to enter in at the strait gate: for many, I say unto you, will seek to enter in, and shall not be able."

—Luke 13:2

As I meditated on this verse, a vivid moving scene 'appeared' on my closed eyelids. Thousands of people milled about the floor inside a vast, squatty hourglass. I hovered anxiously above the neck and urged them to come higher, because I knew something was about to happen and around me was a wide area with plenty of room. They all ignored my pleas.

Suddenly, an event caused the crowd to panic. They began climbing on each others' shoulders to reach the narrow neck, which was about ten feet above the floor. A small number made it through the neck, but most were shoved aside by the more aggressive ones. I watched in horror as some fell to the floor and were trampled. I realized the vision was urging me to share the gospel of eternal life with boldness.

We are living in the last days, and Jesus is the only way to Heaven. It seems that relatively few people understand that truth. Some will respond when we share the gospel, but not nearly as many as we would like. Perhaps the rest will remember the message and enter God's kingdom after our lives on this earth are over.

Dear Father, thank You for offering salvation to all people. Please pour Your love through me to reach people with Your truth, one heart at a time.

Does Anyone Care?

By Bill Larmore

Bible Reading: I Peter 5:6-7

"Casting all your care upon him; for he careth for you."

—I Peter 5:7

In times of trial, I tend to pray earnestly for others, but far less for myself. I have always disliked involving others, even God, in the small difficulties encountered in my even smaller life. If I am miserable, why make those around me feel the same way?

It seems that I was born with a "gift of laughter" and a sense that "the world is mad." I would rather laugh than weep. But recently my quirk sadly betrayed me.

My wife and I were at church. As usual, after the service I was attempting to appear noble and inspiring, when I tripped and fell down right in front of God and everyone. The floor broke my fall, but I immediately became an object of great and bustling public concern.

As I was spread out on the sanctuary floor, unable to remember any jokes and feeling very clumsy, old, and alone, a small voice tickled my ears. The voice said, "Are you all right, Mister Bill? I love you."

The voice was that of the young son of our pastor. Next to him was my beloved wife, and behind her—bending solicitously over the disaster scene—were the anxious, loving faces of members of my church family. God was teaching me a great lesson—one that the Apostle Peter had learned. God does not mean for any of His own to become an island.

Dearest Father God, please help Your own understand that Christians wrapped up in themselves make very small packages.

What's Your Worth?

By Jack G. Elder

Bible Reading: Matthew 10:29-31

"Fear ye not therefore, ye are of more value than many sparrows."
—Matthew 10:31

In America's early days, an old wanted poster might have read: Wanted–Jesse James for train robbery; Reward–$1,000 dead or alive. Jesse was only worth $1,000 to society.

Today, the health insurance industry puts a value not only on a life, but also on body parts—a hand is worth $25,000, or a leg, $50,000.

Maybe you woke up this morning and felt like you weren't worth two cents. You have immeasurable value to the Lord, however. If He watches a sparrow fall, and He says you are worth much more than a sparrow, He is also watching over you. Life is precious, and you are worth far too much to be feeling worthless.

A $20 bill is worth the same whether it's crispy new or crumpled, torn, and dirty. You may be feeling crumpled and torn, but you are still worth everything to the God who created you in His image.

Don't let anyone say you are worthless. Don't accept that comment. God thought you were so valuable that He sent His Son to die for you, to redeem you from worthlessness, and to make you a valuable treasure.

A treasure is only worth what someone is willing to pay for it. A Greek urn might sell for $10,000 to a collector. Imagine the price God was willing to pay for you. It is beyond calculation. You are the most valuable person on this planet. Your value is not in what you do, but in whom you have put your faith, hope, and trust.

Lord, help me get beyond self-worth and self-esteem to God-worth. Help me realize my true worth in Your kingdom.

God's Wonderful Protection

By Judy Becker

*Bible Reading: Psalm 71:1-5; Psalm18:2;
Psalm 61:3; Psalm 144:2*

"Be thou my strong habitation, whereunto I may continually resort: thou hast given commandment to save me; for thou *art* my rock and my fortress."

—Psalm 71:3

To live in Christ is to live in a secure place. Security sets the heart at rest and brings peace. True peace eludes the world. Paul described Christianity to the worldly intellectual Athenians in the language of their own poets. He told them that we Christians "live and move and have our being" in Christ. They listened until he mentioned the resurrection; then most of them scoffed.

God also gives us protection. The LORD is our fortress and a strong high tower. In distant times, towers provided protection against enemies. High above the surrounding plain, the defenders sent arrows to the vulnerable army below.

In 1998, I visited such a tower in the ancient city of Palmyra. Made of stone, it rose three stories high with arrow slits at several levels. It stands as a 1725-year-old vestige to Queen Zenobia's last battle. She had rebelled against Rome's Emperor Aurelian by taking the nations from Egypt to Turkey away from the Roman Empire. Aurelian defeated and pursued her armies back to Palmyra, but the queen further embarrassed him by causing a long siege—probably because of her towers and world famous archers—before she succumbed.

Like the queen's towers, our God is a strong fortress—one which cannot be defeated. Of whom then, shall we be afraid?

O God, help me remember that I have a secure place in You. When the trials of life come, let me not fear, but hold up the shield of faith and trust in Your promises.

The Great Commission

By Judy Parrott

"Heal the sick, cleanse the lepers, raise the dead, cast out devils; freely you have received, freely give."

—Matthew 10:8

Alicia has dedicated her whole life to God, and signs and wonders follow her. A ninety-four-year-old man had a grotesque cancerous growth the size of a melon on his face. Relatives asked Alicia to pray for the Lord to take the man to heaven, but she knew the man wasn't ready for heaven.

God spoke to Alicia and said, "I want to give life. Do not see him in the flesh."

Alicia anointed the man with oil and was amazed to hear him yell, "Bless God!" God healed and instantly saved the man. The growth disappeared beneath Alicia's hand.

The Bible says the anointing (divine empowerment) breaks the yoke. God promised such power to those that would believe. In the Biblical context, *believe* is an action verb. There is a form of godliness in the world, but a general denial of this kind of power. That power comes when nothing matters more than our relationship with God.

True humility is a key that opens doors for us. The statement that pleases God most is when we say we are saved, sanctified, and going to heaven because Jesus paid the price for our sins, not because we did anything to deserve it.

Dear Father in Heaven, reveal to me the form of godliness that has the power to change me and my world. I humble myself before You and ask You to mold me into whatever You want me to become. I give You praise for setting the captives free, for healing the sick, and for giving hope to us all.

The Traveler

By June Parks

Bible Reading: Matthew 18:1-6

"Suffer the little children to come unto me, and forbid them not: for of such is the kingdom of God."

—Mark 10:14b

My friend, Shirley, and her three beautiful towheads had attended the entire week of revival meetings in their little church. After Shirley and her oldest daughter, Tracy, had discussed the matter thoroughly, Tracy had told her mom that she was ready to give her life to Christ.

At the Friday night meeting, Suzanne, the middle daughter, sat happily on her mom's lap, checking out the proceedings. Leighanne, the youngest, sat on one side of Shirley with her thumb in her mouth. That kept her happy. Tracy sat next to Shirley on the other side.

At the end of the service, the preacher extended the invitation for salvation as the congregation slowly sang, "Just As I Am." Tracy and her mom nodded to one another, and as the two had previously agreed, Tracy got up, and with a big smile, walked down the aisle.

Leighanne immediately perked up and asked, "Where is Tracy going?"

When Shirley proudly replied, "Tracy is going to give her life to Christ so she can go to heaven when she dies," Leighanne let out a wail that could be heard all over the sanctuary. Through her sobs she said, "Tracy gets to go everywhere!"

Dear Lord, how wonderful it is when children come into the fold. Please bless children everywhere and keep them close to You.

JESUS LIVES

By Gail Pallotta

Bible Reading: II Corinthians 4:11–18

"While we look not at the things which are seen, but at the things which are not seen: for the things which are seen *are* temporal; but the things which are not seen *are* eternal."

—II Corinthians 4:18

The people who lived on earth and knew and loved Jesus at the time of His crucifixion must have asked themselves some of the same questions we ask today when we experience a tragedy. Why did this happen? How could this happen?

They found themselves on life's tumultuous shore like a beachcomber who stands in the sand focusing on a storm on the horizon because his eyes can't see the sunshine on the other side. But when Jesus rose from the dead, He fulfilled words they really hadn't heard and brought before them glory their eyes hadn't seen, giving them faith, hope, and a promise that He would stay with them forever.

Jesus lives today, working His miracles among us in ways we don't understand and coming to comfort us—if we let Him—when the adversities of an imperfect world afflict us.

To receive His blessings, we must have faith to ask for them and to believe that He answers our prayers, even when we don't consider His response appropriate. Although we sometimes still experience the storm, feeling His presence lightens our burden with the warmth of His love and the hope of better things to come.

Lord, give me faith to live each day looking for Your help and trusting in Your love.

The Spiritually Healthy Heart

By Brenda Thompson Ward

Bible Reading: Ephesians 4:23-32

"Let all bitterness, and wrath, and anger, and clamor, and evil speaking, be put away from you, with all malice."

—Ephesians 4:31

It is easy to become upset when someone says or does something that offends you. Twenty-four years ago, my husband and I left our first ministry in a Christian school and church with heavy hearts. That first venture into the ministry was a great disappointment to us.

After we moved to a new ministry and settled into our positions, I began to have joint pains and other related symptoms. My doctor, after many examinations, began to ask questions about my state of mind. It became apparent that I was harboring bitterness and anger toward two people at our first ministry. What was thought to be the beginning of severe arthritis was actually being caused by my deep anger, bitterness, wrath, and evil-speaking.

No medication could heal my symptoms. It was an illness of the heart. I had to admit that I had so much hatred and malice in my heart that it was affecting my mental and physical health. The only remedy was to make things right with the Lord and with the people with whom I was angry. I went to those people and confessed my harsh feelings. Together we made things right.

That experience taught me how important it is to go to the Lord when I am upset. He is the only one who can help.

Lord, thank You for the life lessons You have taught me. I now realize I cannot control what others say or do, but I can, with Your help, control my thoughts. Please help me keep my heart focused on You.

The Jesus I Knew

By M.L. Anderson

Bible Reading: Psalm 78:4

"We will not hide *them* from their children, shewing to the generation to come the praises of the Lord, and his strength, and his wonderful works that he hath done."

—Psalm 78:4

In 2001, Hollywood prepared to release the film *Pearl Harbor,* and media hoopla involved interviewing the few remaining sailors who had served during the 1941 attack. Rookie reporters seemed eager to tell their own version of what had happened. When the war vets interrupted, "that's not quite the way it happened. What really happened was…" The interviewers yanked the microphone away and continued with their version. Those Pearl Harbor veterans will one day leave this world, and their truth will be left behind. Who will keep our future history books honest?

"Multitudes" of people knew Jesus as a man. They saw Him perform miracles and heard His words. Even after His resurrection, hundreds of people saw Jesus still in human form. Seventy years after Jesus' death, people that had actually known Jesus as a man still roamed Israel. One by one, those people died. When there were none left on earth, His truth was left exposed and vulnerable. The Christians who remained had a charge to keep. They were to be disciples and disseminate truth to their future generations and to all nations. .

I've heard it said that truth becomes legend and legend becomes myth. We cannot allow Jesus to become a legend or a myth under our watch. It is our turn to carry the truth to future generations. We have a charge to keep.

Father, instill in me a passion for those who will come behind me. Help me be faithful, so they will know Your truths.

Personal Testimony

By Brenda Thompson Ward

Bible Reading: I Peter 2:9-20

"Having your conversation honest among the Gentiles: that, whereas they speak against you as evildoers, they may by *your* good works, which they shall behold, glorify God in the day of visitation."

—I Peter 2:12

I used to say I did not care what other people thought of me, but that was the wrong attitude for me to have as a professing Christian. Every day I come into contact with people who don't know the Lord, and my conduct is important. I might be the closest thing to a Bible they see.

Our personal conduct should be Christlike, so that when people mention our name, it will be in a complimentary way. Years ago, while my husband was in school training for a ministry, a wise pastor gave him some most important instructions. His words were simple, but straight to the point. He said, "Remember, be sweet."

It is not always easy to be nice to every person you meet. Some people are unhappy with their lives and some are angry and reactionary. We cannot always know what is going on in another person's mind, but we should always try to be sensitive to the needs and feelings of others.

If we live with those three little words, "Remember, be sweet," in our minds, and if we practice those words, people will have to lie to say something negative about us.

Lord, I pray that You will help me remember daily that there are people who are suffering and in need of a kind word of love and encouragement. Let Your love shine through me so that I can be a walking Bible wherever I go.

Wait on the Lord

By Bill Larmore

Bible Reading: Isaiah 40:30-31

"But they that wait upon the Lord shall renew *their* strength; they shall mount up with wings as eagles; they shall run and not be weary; and they shall walk and not faint."

—Isaiah 40:31

I sit in a hospital waiting room and remember God's ageless words of strength and comfort. The atmosphere is one of apprehension and fear. I am here to visit an old friend whose condition may be terminal, so my heart is heavy.

Thankfully, faith and prayer are also here. I see lips silently moving and humble heads bowed to God amid the harshness of forced laughter and drink-machine rattle. Behind other faces—controlled lonely masks of private pain—I see only sad, incoherent questioning.

In the garish cell, reeking of antiseptic, sweat, deodorant, and heartache, the chairs are rough with the memory of old suffering. I rest uncomfortably in mine—the one with the knife cut on the red, leather arm. My heart grows heavier.

Then, like a stinging wake-up slap across my being, this word comes from God, "Enough! Look to Me!" In shame, I receive His warning.

My strength had dwindled towards empty, as those who had no hope. Weeds of doubt had taken root in my heart, where He had planted faith.

God promised His children that His great power would flow into them. When the weight of darkness introduces despair, as is my case this morning, I first have to pray, then wait patiently for His will to be revealed. We will never be disappointed. Like eagles, we shall soar upon God's mighty wings above the most shattering trials of life.

Dear Father, thank You for teaching my earthbound spirit to fly.

Still Waters

By Bonnie Greenwood Grant

Bible Reading: Psalm 23

"He maketh me to lie down in green pastures: he leadeth me beside the still waters."

—Psalm 23:2

My Aunt Jo has a small, white poodle that looks like a sheered sheep in the summer. The dog, Camilla, didn't like to walk near the lake. My aunt couldn't understand why. Most dogs liked to cool off when the sun was beating down. But not Camilla; she kept trying to lure her mistress back up the hill, away from the water.

"I can't understand why she dislikes water," Jo said.

"Maybe she's like a sheep," I said. "I'm told they are afraid of turbulent water because their wool absorbs so much water they can get water-logged and drown. Maybe Camilla's fur absorbs water like a sheep's, and she's afraid of drowning."

"Or maybe," Jo said with a sudden knowing grin, "it's because I threw her in the lake to cool her off the last time we were here."

The mystery had been solved. What my aunt had meant for blessing had created fear in Camilla.

If we let God guide us, we do not need to fear. He will fulfill all our needs and protect us from harm. He will give us the best because He knows our innermost desires, fears, and concerns; He will lead us where we can satisfy those needs safely.

Lord, You are my shepherd, and You refresh my soul. Thank You.

Satan's Lies

By Brenda Thompson Ward

Bible Reading: Genesis 3

"And when the woman saw that the tree *was* good for food, and that it *was* pleasant to the eyes, and a tree to be desired to make *one* wise, she took of the fruit thereof, and did eat, and gave also unto her husband with her; and he did eat."

—Genesis 3:6

Satan uses many methods to complete his madness. He often mixes lies with truth to make things look believable. Satan appealed to Eve's senses when he tempted her. She looked at the tree and saw that it was good for food (lust of the flesh), pleasant to the eye (lust of the eye), and to be desired to make one wise (pride of life).

Everything seemed innocent enough. What could it hurt to take a small taste of the fruit? Like many, Eve made her first mistake when she listened to the voice of Satan. Satan deceived Eve, and Adam joined in her sin.

It only took a split second for Adam and Eve to realize they had made a tremendous mistake. They didn't have the great experience they had expected. Instead, they received a complete knowledge of good and evil. The consequences of their actions brought guilt, a feeling they had never experienced before. Along with the loss of innocence, they had to live with the consequences of their actions—God drove them from the Garden.

All of us can fall short of the glory of God. No person is exempt. Daily, we must live close to the Lord, keeping our eyes steadfastly on Him and praying for the strength to recognize and refuse Satan's lies.

Thank You for Your Word, my daily instruction. Help me guard my heart with Your Word to keep me from sin.

God's Garden of Life

By Darlene Applegate

Bible Reading: Genesis 2:1-8

"And the Lord God planted a garden eastward in Eden; and there he put the man whom he had formed."

—Genesis 2:8

A season came when I was separated from my husband through death. It felt like a monsoon, as rain pounded down on me. I longed to hear Richard's voice and to cuddle close, wrapped in the security of his arms. But I knew that would no longer be possible in this life.

Uprooted, I faced many challenges. The Lord came to my place in His garden and asked, "Why do you weep?"

"I miss my husband, Lord."

"He is with me, and I am with you," He replied. "My Father's house has many rooms, and there is much to do inside and out. But when I heard you weeping, I came to comfort you. I will not let the waters rise above your head nor will I allow grief to overcome you. You will not be pulled from My garden of life. I will wrap My arms around you and in Me you will find security."

"I am angry with You, Lord. If You had willed, Richard would not have died."

"I am not angry with you. I am loving and patient. In Me he lives, so he is not dead. You have learned much, but still have much to learn. Continue to walk with Me. I want to show you a new field."

As I am living in God's garden of life, I am learning spiritual lessons that will uplift my faith and sustain my life for the rainy seasons to come.

Thank You, Lord, for Your loving-kindness and for the newness of each day in Your garden of life.

Winters

By Gail Pallotta

Bible Reading: Isaiah 42: 6-17

"Behold, the former things are come to pass, and new things do I declare: before they spring forth I tell you of them."

—Isaiah 42:9

Where I grew up at the foothills of the North Carolina mountains, winter brought cold, icy winds. The hills stripped of their foliage appeared barren. The trees swayed like skeletons with scraggly gray arms, looking as though they could barely exist in the harsh weather. Eventually, snow covered them, causing their branches to sag.

I sometimes think I am barren like those trees in winter. Then suddenly, I realize I've struggled through a day, a week, or even a month, trying to make it on my own. Even though Christ came long ago, giving our lives new meaning and showing us how to love, sometimes I go about my daily routine without Him. I imagine on such occasions I'm similar to some of the biblical characters who lived before Jesus' time. While I'm not breaking any laws, I'm also not putting my trust in Christ. At those times, it helps to step back from my hectic lifestyle to stop and remember His sacrifice of unconditional love.

Always in the mountains in the spring, leaves and apple blossoms bring a fresh start to the trees. When I see their unfailing glory appear once again, it reminds me that Christ is always there for me.

Dear Lord, thank You for sending Your Son. Help me accept the love You give every day of my life.

Change Your Thinking — Your Mind

By Charlene Elder

Bible Reading: Romans 12

"I beseech you therefore, brethren, by the mercies of God, that ye present your bodies a living sacrifice, holy, acceptable unto God, *which* is your reasonable service. And be not conformed to this world: but be ye transformed by the renewing of your mind, that ye may prove what *is* that good, and acceptable, and perfect, will of God."

—Romans 12:1-2

I once heard about a family whose children were severely handicapped—not physically, but mentally and emotionally—because their mother continually told them they were worthless and stupid. When the principal at the school became aware of the family situation, he asked the teachers how they taught those troubled children.

Some teachers hadn't recognized the problem, but several teachers reported that the children were doing well in their classes. The principal concluded that the children had higher scores and acted better with teachers who gave them positive reinforcement. The troubled students had learned to think differently about themselves—their minds had been renewed. They had received positive feedback from their teachers and had gained self-worth and acceptance, which was evidenced in their work.

God tells us not to conform to the world's way of thinking, but to *renew* our minds with His Word daily so we know His good, acceptable, and perfect will. We should not think as the world thinks (with greed, selfishness, anger, or anxiety). We should renew our minds according to God's Word in order to enjoy peace, joy, and life everlasting.

Lord, help me renew my mind according to Your Word. Let me think like You think, and let me be an encourager to others who haven't yet had their minds renewed.

Chipmunks

By Brenda Thompson Ward

Bible Reading: Genesis 1:24-25

"And God said, Let the earth bring forth the living creature after his kind, cattle, and creeping thing, and beast of the earth after his kind: and it was so."

—Genesis 1:24

My favorite time of the day is right after the sun begins to rise. I awaken around five in the morning and go out on the back porch as soon as the light begins to peek through the dark.

My yard is full of God's little creatures. There are more squirrels than I can count and all sorts of birds, including three mourning doves. There were four doves, but a neighborhood cat murdered one. Since doves mate for life, there is now a lonely dove and a dove couple. There are also three beautiful lizards that change colors when they sunbathe. I make sure that all of those little creatures are well fed.

The most interesting critters to me are the chipmunks. There are three in our yard: Harry, Barry, and Larry. I've enjoyed showing my grandchildren the small hole in the ground that is the entrance into their home. Those three chipmunks amaze me because they are up and busy before the other creatures are up. I've placed a bird feeder on my picnic table for them. If I'm quiet and don't move, they climb on the table and feast on the manna I have provided.

This morning, watching those amazing little creatures made me feel guilty about my laziness at home and in the Lord's work. If I were as productive as the chipmunks and worked without complaining and whining, I would be a more productive servant for the Lord.

Lord, thank You for using Your creation to show me the importance of being diligent in Your work.

The Just Shall Live by Faith

By Judy Becker

Bible Reading: Hebrews 11:24-29

"Blessed is the man that maketh the Lord his trust, and respecteth not the proud, nor such as turn aside to lies."

—Psalm 40:4

Moses was such a man. All the riches and the prominent position afforded him from his upbringing in the royal household did not sway him from following Jehovah. Hebrews 11: 26-27 says, "Esteeming the reproach of Christ greater riches than the treasures in Egypt…by faith he forsook Egypt not fearing the wrath of the king." Nor did he kowtow to the mighty Pharaoh when God sent him back to free His people. Later, when the proud people turned aside to worship a false god—turning aside to lies—God removed their blessing.

If we follow Moses' example, we too will meet the proud and those who speak lies loudly. I think of the atheists who raise a voice unafraid, the abortionists who lie and deny that the unborn are human, and the evolutionists who dispute God's creation. Are we afraid of those proud liars? No! We see them as signs of the end of the age.

We live by faith, like Moses. We see the ungodly leaders of this world defy God's Word, and we laugh, yes laugh, as Psalm 52:6 says we will, because we know their final end. We walk in His promise to save the righteous from His wrath upon the proud. The just shall walk by faith.

Lord God, bolster my faith. Keep me strong in You, that I may stand against the proud liars of today. Let me not be silent or afraid, but stand up for You. Let me look for those greater riches that Moses sought.

The Repairer

By Jack G. Elder

Bible Reading: Isaiah 58:6-12

"And *they that shall be* of thee shall build the old waste places: thou shalt raise up the foundations of many generations; and thou shalt be called, The repairer of the breach, The restorer of paths to dwell in."

—Isaiah 58:12

Most of us watched in shock as Katrina hit the US Southern coast on August 29, 2005. Katrina was the costliest and one of the deadliest hurricanes in the history of the United States. It was the sixth-strongest Atlantic hurricane ever recorded and the third-strongest hurricane on record that made landfall in the United States.

The most severe loss of life and property damage occurred when the devastating storm breached the levees that protected the lower elevation in New Orleans. Even though many people have worked hard to repair and restore that area after the storm, there is much more to repair.

Every day storms hit individual lives with equally devastating results. They may be real storms, or they might be thunderstorms of illness, rainstorms of the death of a loved one, whirlwinds of a child involved in criminal activity, or tornados of lost work. Many around us are hurting.

God has called us to be repairers and restorers to those who are suffering from the storms of life. People need hope, encouragement, and yes, help with physical needs. We can be a restorer of love in a loveless society—a repairer of broken hearts and shattered dreams.

God calls us the repairers and the restorers. He needs us to help others on His Home Improvement Team.

Help us, Father, to be observant of the needs of others, knowing that many are suffering from the storms of life.

Out of the Comfort Zone

By Judy Parrott

Bible Reading: Matthew 14:22-36

"And He said, Come. And when Peter was come down out of the ship, he walked on the water, to go to Jesus."

—Matthew 14:29

I can imagine the disciples rowing all night after a hard day of serving over five thousand people. The wind sucked up huge waves, rolling them over the ship hour after tedious hour. Perhaps the exhausted men were grumbling and filled with doubts, thinking *Where is Jesus when we need Him? Will we ever make it to the other side alive?*

Suddenly, a phantom appeared standing on the crest of a wave. They were terrified, then greatly relieved when they heard His voice saying, "Be of good cheer. It is I. Be not afraid."

Peter got excited. He never tired of miracles. "If it be thou, bid me to come..." he said.

"Come," Jesus responded. (Don't you think Jesus was delighted to see Peter's faith?)

Peter walked on the water until he took his eyes off Jesus and let his logic take over; but at least he'd had enough faith to get out of the boat.

Jesus said to the men, "Oh, ye of little faith." Was He talking to all of them? What did it take for Him to convince the disciples that nothing was impossible? Their hearts remained hardened whenever times got tough—until the Holy Spirit arrived.

Dear Lord, life is so exciting when I get out of my comfort zone. Please help me step onto the water in faith and walk with You wherever You want me to go. I thank You that faith is a gift You have given me to use in this great commission. I am ready to go—send me.

SHE DID WHAT SHE COULD

By Brenda Thompson Ward

Bible Reading: Mark 14:3-9

"She hath done what she could: she is come aforehand to anoint my body to the burying."

—Mark 14:8

My husband and I have been involved in church ministries for almost thirty years, and I have been faithful in our church since the early years of our marriage. However, that did not prepare me for the extra hours required to work in the church as a staff member. It was not that I hadn't been told about that aspect of the ministry; but it is one thing to hear it and another to live it.

Today, our world operates on a fast track. Sometimes, it is difficult to keep up. When that happens, I find myself complaining and asking, "What about time for me?" I realize—even before the words escape my lips—that my attitude is one of selfishness. That I am placing my own desires above what the Lord wants from me. My complaint is an unloving remark.

Everything Mary did was out of her love for the Lord. She wanted to learn as much as she could; she had hunger for the His words. She wanted to bless Jesus. The alabaster box was probably the most expensive possession she owned. Her sacrifice was to give all she had to the Lord. She did what she could! Jesus wanted Mary to be remembered for her sacrifice and dedication. Forever, I will remember Mary and her unselfish actions.

Thank You for the lessons I learn simply by opening Your Word. Help me faithfully seek Your will over mine. Give me a love and concern for others.

Role Model

By Bonnie Greenwood Grant

Bible Reading: Isaiah 3:10-12

"O my people, they which lead thee cause *thee* to err, and destroy the way of thy paths."

—Isaiah 3:12b

Who are our leaders? Who are our role models? Standing in the grocery line, I am flooded with bright pictures and glaring headlines telling about the latest escapades of the rich and famous; telling how they have lost control of their lives; how they are ruled by addictions, are hampered by low IQs, and how they have lost sight of what God has planned for their lives. They have stumbled and lost their way, and we are witnesses of their debacles.

In contrast, I watched a tribute to Ruth Graham; a woman I never knew much about. I doubt if I would have been able to come up with her name if asked, but what a woman she was.

Ruth was born to missionaries in China, was married to Evangelist, Billy Graham, was the mother of five children who are all serving the Lord today, and was buried in a plywood casket built by a murderer.

Ruth Graham lived her life as a true Christian, reaching out to those no one else wanted to deal with. She invited criminals and the homeless to her dinner table. She was the kind of woman I felt sad that I had never known. She was the kind of woman that I would have treasured as a friend. She was a role model of the highest degree.

Jesus, if we can't be leaders ourselves, please guide us to good leaders who will help us find the path to You.

Beauty From Within

By Brenda Thompson Ward

Bible Reading: I Peter 3:1-4

"But *let it be* the hidden man of the heart, in that which is not corruptible, *even the ornament* of a meek and quiet spirit, which is in the sight of God of great price."

—I Peter 3:4

Although this passage speaks about the husband and wife relationship, the words also describe a characteristic every Christian should possess. To be meek and quiet does not mean one must go through a personality change. If that were true, I would be up the proverbial creek without a paddle. However, the passage speaks about our attitude toward others.

Have you ever met someone and your immediate reaction was a negative one? I have. Years ago, I worked in a children's ministry with a woman I felt was physically unattractive. Yet, the longer I worked with her and saw her "inner woman," the more beautiful she became to me. After awhile, I did not think about her physical appearance. All I could see was her heart and her dedication to the children.

You cannot purchase that kind of beauty from a cosmetics counter. Such beauty comes from within the heart of a person who is submissive to God and is based on her love and devotion.

A teacher once told me to look at others through the eyes of Jesus. When I look at others with the eyes of the Lord, it is easier to accept them. Jesus sets the example for us by loving us all the same regardless of our physical appearance.

Thank You, Lord, for Your undying love. Help me remember that You do not love one more than another. As I go through the day, help me see others through Your eyes of love.

The Promise

By June Parks

Scripture Reading: Mark 4:8

"And other fell on good ground and did yield fruit that spang up and increased…"

—Mark 4:8

In my usual day as a realtor, I drive a lot. One extremely hot day, in order to feel the fresh breeze on my face, I had my car windows down. That made for a refreshing stop on the bridge as I waited for the light to change to allow me to turn left.

Over to the left, I spotted what has become my life's mantra. I cannot forget it. So simple! In the steaming hot pavement, amongst the sticks, stones, and trash, there was a slim crack. That crack was home to a weed—a tall, thriving, unloved, blooming, beautiful weed.

God had decided on that day, that in that unlikely, barren place I was supposed to enjoy a flower. It was a treat and my sermon for the day—a sermon that said, "If you are as stubborn as a weed, then you can make it."

We are promised no more than a *toehold* on this earth—the rest is up to us. That is God's promise. If we bury our roots deeply and reach up for the sunshine, the heavens, God's blessings, and all of the good things in life, then we will become tough, hardworking, and beautiful in this life. God gives us the tools and the opportunities, but we must do the performing.

If we just keep slugging, we will bloom!

Dear Lord, grant me the ability and the pleasure to see big things in the minutiae—the promise in every day and everything. Keep me smiling when I recognize small miracles because life is my miracle and my joy.

The Worst Words

By Bill Larmore

Bible Reading: Matthew 26:73-75

"Then began he to curse and to swear, *saying* "I know not the man."
—Matthew 26:74

Christian, suppose you were hanging a picture and you hit your thumb with a hammer. Would you calmly exclaim, "Gracious me," or might your involuntary response be a descriptive epithet from your unsaved vocabulary? That happened one morning long ago to a big fisherman named Peter. *His finger of faith* was smashed with the world's hammer of hate. He was accused of a criminal action for following Jesus, and his feelings were in torment.

Only hours before on the Mount of Olives, he had assured his beloved master of perfect faithfulness, even if all other disciples deserted him. But now, Peter could not grasp what had happened. Jesus, his rock and his direction, the man who called Almighty God "Father," the man who calmed storms, healed lepers, raised the dead, walked on water, and was his superman…had been arrested for blasphemy like a common criminal.

The attack on Peter's faith was numbing. When accosted as a Jesus disciple, he had reverted to being a fisherman. He cursed and denied the association. Yet in the midst of torture, Jesus looked upon Peter with forgiveness and love. Peter wept bitterly, repented of his traitor feelings, and years later died for his Lord and Savior.

Well, that was Peter, 2,000 years ago. So what does ancient history mean to me today? Just this: I cannot trust my unsettled feelings either. I learn from the past, but I must also weep bitterly in repentance. I pray to God that I will never revert to mindless fear and ungodly selfishness.

Dear Father, I pray that I will always portray Your feelings and not my own.

The Ripple Effect

By Jack G. Elder

Bible Reading: Colossians 3:15-17

"And whatsoever ye do in word or deed, *do* all in the name of the Lord Jesus, giving thanks to God and the Father by him."

—Colossians 3:17

We have all thrown a stone into a pond and watched the rippling rings travel out from the center. Likewise, with our life's influence in the world, we have set into motion rings to those around us. Those rings can be good or bad. Good rings like peace, joy, and generosity go out to help others. Bad rings like strife, hatred, and stinginess carry hurt to others.

One good act of kindness can have a far-reaching effect, just as the stone thrown into the water causes rings to go across the pond. It is a reminder that we are not alone in this world. Everyone throws in their stones, and concentric circles go out from each one causing them to mingle. Some spheres add to each other, making a greater ring and having a larger effect, while others subtract, almost halting the ripples.

Acts of kindness and generosity make circles that generate love and hope. What we say is like a stone dropped into the world around us. It causes gentle ripples of reconciliation and understanding to others, or waves that rock another person's world and shatter their hope and happiness.

We all create many splashes in our lives. We need to remember how much our lives influence others and make a strong effort to create ripples that bring healing.

Father, help me affect the world around me in positive, helpful ways today. Let my influence be a reflection of Your love for the world You created.

Author and Finisher

By Susan M. Watkins

Bible Reading: Philippians 1:3-7

"Being confident of this very thing, that he which hath begun a good work in you will perform *it* until the day of Jesus Christ."

—Philippians 1:6

The end result. It takes divine eyes to capture that view. I strain to locate the finished product and question its existence; He sees with satisfied clarity.

I personally rejoice in God's "last name." "Omega." It perfectly balances "Alpha." Letter for letter, vision for vision. What He begins, He finishes.

His covenant is tightly bound to His conception. What we initiate has no promise. Only His inertia is joined to the finish line. Our confidence is released by His steadfast history interlaced with mankind. Eons of meticulous documentation echoes His faithfulness toward us.

We are tempted to scratch our heads and say, "It can't be done." His compassions delightfully prove us wrong. There is no mountain too high, no pit too deep, no desert too dry, no report too devastating. God in all His glory is already there.

This verse offers seven promises: Confidence in God's abilities; His authorship; His interaction; His good works; His choice to display His power in us; His promise of completion; and His covenant to continue with future generations.

No matter where life finds us—no matter how daunting the task, how discouraging the news, how dark the night—God lovingly surrounds us with hope, light, and direction. He alone is capable and deserving of the name, "Beginning AND End." He is not, "Beginning, but now I quit." No! He puts a very concrete period at the end of our open questions. He views the end from the beginning. If your situation calls for an expert opinion…consult our Omnipotent God.

Father, unfold Your plan before my eyes.

Sing Praise

By Bonnie Greenwood Grant

Bible Reading: Isaiah 12:1-6

"Sing unto the Lord; for he hath done excellent things: this *is* known in all the earth. Cry out and shout, thou inhabitant of Zion: for great *is* the Holy One of Israel in the midst of thee."

—Isaiah 12:5-6

Before we moved to Georgia, I was in a prayer group. Each prayer warrior had a notebook beside the phone in which they wrote the name of the person requesting prayer, the prayer itself, the date of the request, and the date the prayer was answered. God always answered our prayers. Sometimes the answer was "no," but the answer always turned out to be in our best interest.

One prayer warrior's husband was the golf pro at a city-operated golf course. One city official wanted the man to divert city funds into the official's pocket. The official tried everything in his power to 'persuade' him.

Our prayer group prayed and prayed, but the date answered column stayed empty. Two or three days before the four-year mark, the official was found out, fired, and banished. Having the *date answered column* proved God's faithfulness. Often we forgot we had prayed for something, so writing in the date served as a gentle reminder.

My oldest daughter frequently requested prayer. Whenever she had a test coming up, she put herself on the prayer line. We prayed faithfully. One day, she called and was a little upset. "Didn't you pray for me?" she asked. "I got a B+ on my test."

"Yes, we prayed for you to do your best," I replied.

"Mom; no. Pray for A's." she responded.

Sweet Lord, thank You for loving me. Please help me see the marvelous things You do for me every day. I thank You for them.

Who's Your Daddy?

By Jack G. Elder

Bible Reading: Romans 8:14-17

"For ye have not received the spirit of bondage again to fear; but ye have received the Spirit of adoption, whereby we cry, Abba, Father. The Spirit itself beareth witness with our spirit, that we are the children of God."

—Romans 8:15-16

Who's your daddy? Everyone has a dad. Maybe you didn't know your real father, or he died when you were young. Hopefully, you had a good rapport with your father, but possibly you had a troubling relationship. Fathers can disappoint as well as nurture and encourage. No father is perfect.

Part of your Christian benefits package is becoming a child of God. The Holy Spirit, whom God gave you at your new birth, bears witness in your heart that you are now one of God's special children. He is now your heavenly Father. He is perfect. He will never let you down and will always encourage and strengthen you to live the life He desires for you.

God gave you the Spirit of adoption, not the Spirit of fear. Having a Father like the creator of all things can free you from the fears of bondage to this world and its chaotic inconsistency. You never know what to expect from the world, but you can know what to expect from an unchanging Father who loves and cares for you.

Now is the time to get to know your Daddy. Jesus said, "If you see me, you have seen the Father." The Father wrote you a letter telling about Himself and gave you the pathway to true success. Read the letter—the Word. Get to know your Daddy.

Heavenly Father, thank You for being my Daddy and for helping me be a child who will make You proud.

WAIT FOR GOD'S DIRECTION

By Patty Rocco

Bible Reading: John 19:26-27; I Samuel 30

"When Jesus therefore saw his mother, and the disciple standing by, whom he loved, he saith unto his mother, Woman, behold thy son!"

—John 19:26

When we experience tragedy, God sometimes gives us something to do. As John stood grieving at the foot of the Cross, Christ gave him the responsibility of taking care of his mother, Mary. It may not have been what John thought was most important, but it was most important to Christ.

In I Samuel 30, David and his men returned to their hometown of Ziklag. To their horror, their homes were charred ruins, and the Amalekites had kidnapped their family members. The grieving men wanted to stone David.

In verse 6 of I Samuel 30 we read, "David strengthened himself in the Lord." He inquired of the Lord, and God gave him something to do. He sent David to recover his family and the families of his men. Not only was every person recovered alive, but God blessed David and his men with a huge amount of plunder.

When tragedy strikes, we may be tempted to throw stones at God. We may think that His direction for us is menial and worthless. However, our best recourse is to obey Him. God proved that He could take our railings when His Son, Jesus, hung on the cross, giving His life a ransom for our sins. Such love demands that we obediently follow His directions.

Thank You, Father, for the wonder of the Cross. Thank You, Jesus, for the work You accomplished there. Thank You, Holy Spirit, for directing my steps and allowing me to be strengthened in You.

A Man Who Pleased God

By Brenda Thompson Ward

Bible Reading: Job 1:1-12

"There was a man in the land of Uz, whose name *was* Job; and that man was perfect and upright, and one that feared God, and eschewed evil."

—Job 1:1

Job lived his life doing the right things, and God was pleased with him. One day, God declared to Satan that Job was a unique man because "there was none like him in the earth." Wow! My thought when I read that was *what would God be saying to Satan if they were looking down on me as I went through my days?*

Recently, I had a very frustrating day. It seems that every time my husband goes out of town, something at home breaks. This time while he was away, my dryer quit working. I had two baskets of wet clothes and no way to dry them. My reactions to the circumstances beyond my control were anger and frustration. I even remarked aloud, "Lord, I don't need this!"

Later, I began a three-week study on the man, Job. The study brought things into perspective. I began to see that nothing happens in my life that I cannot handle with God's help. I realized that my "little inconvenience" was nothing when compared to what Job lived and suffered through.

For me to get upset and angry about a machine breaking was ridiculous. The Lord spoke to me through His Word and awakened my mind and heart to the fact that on the radar screen of important things and crisis situations in life, my dryer problem was only a tiny bleep.

Lord, please help me distinguish real problems from minor inconveniences. Help me seek and trust You in every situation of life.

Whom Should We Fear?

By Marcus Beavers

Bible Reading: Luke 12:1-5

"But I will forewarn you whom ye shall fear: Fear him, which after he hath killed hath power to cast into hell; yea, I say to you, Fear him."

—Luke 12:5

Many modern philosophers and scientists have assured us that we don't have to fear God. Their faith is in the impersonal—along with time and chance—which never explains why there is specific form and order in the universe and in the personality of man.

People were amazed by the teachings and miracles of Christ. He spoke with tremendous authority. As God the Eternal Son, He had knowledge of ultimate things. Jesus warned against the Pharisees, who thought their religious ways and knowledge were enough.

Being religiously convinced is not enough. Our worldview must reflect God's truth about the world. True science and philosophy are helpful, but are limited in scope. Jesus says God will judge every person. Isn't it interesting that Christ, who loves and saves sinners, is also the strongest preacher of hell in the entire Bible?

Godly fear involves respect, honor, and an attitude of thankfulness to the one true God. God gives us the answers we need in His revelation, the Bible. That is where we must look to understand Whom we should fear.

Father in Heaven, Creator of all things, please forgive my lack of godly fear. Please create in me a clean heart. I want to revere the truth of Your Word. May Your name be hallowed in all the earth, and may Your kingdom come on earth as it is in Heaven.

The Unchanging Heart

By Jack G. Elder

Bible Reading: Psalm 108:1-4

"O God, my heart is fixed; I will sing and give praise, even with my glory."

—Psalm 108:1

When I read this verse for the first time, I thought it meant that the psalmist had experienced a broken heart and because God had intervened with his healing power, God had fixed his heart. That is the amazing thing about the Word. His Words speak to the need, and even if we don't know the Hebrew word for "fixed," it provides healing and life. We don't have to be theologians for the Word to work in our lives. It just seems right that a repaired heart is cause for praise.

An alternate understanding, however, is that the word "fixed" means established, firm, and unchangeable. The Psalmist was not going to let anything sway his thinking and his heart—that inner place of knowing. This is an age when knowledge is expanding at an exponential rate. Scientific research, religious study, and technology are rapidly growing. Nothing seems to remain the same.

In spite of the changes going on in the psalmist's life, he said he had fixed his heart on the Word and would not move from what he knew as the truth, the whole truth, and nothing but the truth.

When we open the newspaper, we never know what changes took place in our world overnight. When we open the Bible, we know God has not changed, and He has taken into account all the rapid advances going on around us. Let us fix our heart on Him and praise Him.

Thank You, Father, that You never change. I fix my heart on that promise.

The Power of Comfort

By Susan M. Watkins

Bible Reading: II Corinthians 1:3-5

"Who comforteth us in all our tribulation, that we may be able to comfort them which are in any trouble, by the comfort wherewith we ourselves are comforted of God."

—II Corinthians 1:4

It's the dark side of trial—the sheer silence interrupted only by our cries of "Why, Lord, why?" How hot the furnace is that we each must sometimes face. We never volunteer to enter, yet a confirmed reservation awaits our arrival. Why does God allow such things in the lives of the children He loves?

The above verse provides the answer; it's an obvious secret. The gift of trials serves as a spiritual teacher to explain the depth of God. Trials also strengthen our faith—a necessary muscle that needs development.

Underground treasure is the secondary application of the benefits of tribulation. Upon reemergence, we're qualified to comfort others with the comfort we received from God's arms during our troubles. The Lord promises His tenderness. He never withholds this mothering aspect of His nature.

In the midst of the numerous tragedies I've faced, I was never moved by those who couldn't relate to my situation. Yet when the Lord appointed a fellow-sufferer with the experience and a clear exit point to shadow my path, I listened intently and was stirred. Our shared cross allowed my heart to open to receive another's mirrored comfort. Only valley-walkers with familiar grief were qualified to reach that deep.

When God wipes away our tears of questioning and replaces them with comfort, He expects us to do likewise when we encounter the wounded on the road to Samaria. Power released through comfort must never be overlooked or underestimated.

Lord, allow me to lift another's weary head as You have lifted mine.

Seeing Clearly

By Gail Pallotta

Bible Reading: I Corinthians 13

"For now we see through a glass, darkly; but then face to face: now I know in part; but then shall I know even as also I am known."

—I Corinthians 13:12

Even though we learn in Genesis that we live in a world of sin, Jesus died for us, so we can be forgiven. Even after we accept Christ, we are still surrounded by imperfections such as violence and corruption—we may *even* be victims of those things.

We, too, can act in uncaring ways by ignoring or adding to the pain of others. Our thoughts can become confused, distracting us from Jesus, who is our vision for spiritual guidance and hope.

When I go to the optometrist for a check-up, if he uses the wrong lens, the letters and numbers become blurred. Wanting a good report, I try to see through the fuzziness. However, I can't force correct vision. Nothing appears clear until the doctor finds the right piece of curved glass and adjusts it.

Sometimes I find myself attempting to see through life's hazy dilemmas on my own, instead of putting my faith in Christ and letting Him correct the way I look at them.

Lord, I am so thankful that You sent Jesus, who died for my salvation. Please help me have faith in Him and seek His guidance each day.

This Little Light of Mine

By Jack G. Elder

Bible Reading: Matt 5:14-16

"Let your light so shine before men, that they may see your good works, and glorify your Father which is in heaven."

—Matthew 5:16

I remember the first time I was in total darkness. It was in the Oregon Caves near Cave Junction, Oregon. The tour group I was in climbed down ladders into the caves and wandered around looking at all the wondrous sights—the stalagmites, stalactites, and columns—until we finally came into a large room.

The tour guide then announced that he was about to turn off all the lights and leave us in total darkness. At that, he flipped the switch, and we stood still in absolute darkness. My eyes did not adjust to the darkness; the room remained totally dark. I couldn't see my hand in front of my face.

Then the tour guide lit a small match. The whole cave brightened from the light of that one tiny light. It wasn't as bright as the sun, but it was bright enough for us to see and to move around.

We are like that little match. It may not seem like we put out much light, but in the darkness of the world, it is brilliant. As long as we don't hide our light, but let it shine, we will glorify God through our little light.

Father, help me let my light shine no matter the depths of the darkness or the heights of the trials and doubts. I want to bring You glory through my little light.

The Power of Words

By Brenda Thompson Ward

Bible Reading: Matthew 12:33-37; II Samuel 11:1-27; II Samuel 12:1-24

"For by thy words thou shall be justified, and by thy words, thou shalt be condemned."

—Matthew 12:37

I love words. Without them I would have nothing to say and my life would be extremely dull. I am a woman of many words. Not only do I like to talk; I also love to write.

Words have great power. They have the power to comfort and convey love, and they have the power to curse, to ruin reputations through slander, and to manipulate. People express anger through their words, and they show appreciation through spoken words. Parents use them to train and discipline their children and to warn them of danger.

I remember King David's words after he had sinned with Bathsheba. He paid a high price for what he said—his words were responsible for the death of a faithful soldier, Bathsheba's husband, Uriah, and for the death of David and Bathsheba's first child.

My words have not produced physical death as David's did, but I do recall a time when I misused words by repeating a piece of gossip. I did not say anything harmful or critical, but I did repeat something that was not the truth. I had to repent and go to the person I had gossiped about to ask for forgiveness. Praise God, I was forgiven and restored. It is definitely important how we use our words.

Lord, help me to daily guard my mouth. I don't want to be known as a gossip or a troublemaker. Give me the wisdom to know what to say and when to say it. Please help me use kindness in my speech.

Light Your World

By Robert W. Ellis

Bible Reading: Hebrews 9

"For there was a tabernacle made; the first, wherein *was* the candlestick, and the table, and the shewbread; which is called the sanctuary."

—Hebrews 9:2

I am amazed that after all these years in church I still hear new things from the pastors' sermons that I did not know before. Recently, our youth pastor amazed me yet again with a sermon about the Jerusalem temple articles, primarily the lampstand and the shewbread. He said that during his studies in the Old and New Testaments about these two temple articles, he discovered that the lampstand represented Jesus' church with Jesus, the Light of the World in the center, and the shewbread represented Jesus, the Bread of Life.

The job of the lampstand was to illuminate the shewbread for all that entered the Holy Place. *Wow, that's neat* I thought. I realized that our job as the church is to illuminate Jesus in a dark and dying world. In fact, it is our only job. We can perform that job in many different ways, but all those *ways* should point people to Jesus, the Light of the World and the Bread of Life.

Help me, Lord, to be a light for You and for Your Word. Don't let me get so involved in *jobs*, even in my church, that I don't shine a light on You. Let my light shine only to bring glory to You.

The Conviction of Courage

By Bill Larmore

Bible Reading: II Timothy 1:6-8

"For God hath not given us the spirit of fear; but of power, and of love, and of a sound mind."

—II Timothy 1:7

The apostle Paul, while sending that encouraging admonition to his protégé, Timothy, was in a Roman jail facing a possible death sentence. The average man so positioned would have been obsessed with hiring a cheap lawyer and making his defense. Yet Paul had his mind on something else—a young preacher named Timothy.

Timothy's pastorate in Ephesus had not been easy. His church, trying to place one foot in Heaven and the other in the world, had mocked his youth and inexperience. Also, persecution of Christians was ominously growing in the idol-centered communities. Timothy was apprehensive.

Paul counseled Timothy to straighten up. He was to fearlessly exercise his God-given gifts and graces, and he was not to allow those endowments to grow stale from lack of use. A Christian leader was never meant to be a tragedy of indecision, but rather a powerful, godly example of strength, love, and steadfast resolution. He was to foster within himself the three major characteristics of the true Christian leader: wisdom, strength, and unselfish love.

Those powerful traits are as readily available from God today as they were to Paul and Timothy in AD 66. They are character foundation stones upon which rest God's eternal building of true faith, firm doctrine, endless patience, and everlasting love, which are available to all believers.

Dear Father, when we Christians are arraigned by the world, the charge against us being suspicion of having in our possession Your courage, power, love, and sound mind, please help us to be found *guilty* on all counts.

Widow's Weeds

By Judy Becker

Bible Reading: Deuteronomy 10:18; Psalms 68:5

"The Lord will destroy the house of the proud: but he will establish the border of the widow."

—Proverbs 15:25

As a widow, I struggle to keep my property in good repair. One Sunday as I drove into my driveway after church, I said, "Oh, Lord, just look at those unsightly weeds along the fence. I really don't have time to clear them." The weeds were four to five feet tall.

An inner voice responded, "Well, why don't you just curse them?" I was shocked. *Was that me, or did You just speak to me Lord?* I wasn't sure whose voice it was, but just in case it was God, I decided to obey. I stopped my car, pointed to every weed, and cursed them in the name of Jesus.

The next day while walking to the mailbox, I cursed the weeds again. Each day after that, I examined them closely, expecting them to shrivel like the fig tree Jesus had cursed; but the weeds kept thriving. After a week with no change, I decided I didn't have enough faith.

Several days later, two men came to my house. The older man got out of his truck and said, "You probably don't remember me, but I'm Chris' dad." (Chris had bartered hunting rights with me in exchange for bush hogging my pasture.) "We weren't working today," he continued, "so we came over to clean your fence line."

The men went to work, and when they were finished, the weeds were gone. The weeds have never come back. Praise God! God does things way beyond whatever we ask or think—but He always does it His way.

Father, let me remember this lesson: Your ways are not my ways—they are far better.

The Path of the Just

By Diana J. Baker

Bible Reading: Proverbs 4:14-27

"But the path of the just *is* as the shining light, that shineth more and more unto the perfect day."

—Proverbs 4:18

Each day that we live, we are faced with a choice of pathways. Many choose paths that lead to loneliness, heartbreak and despair. They spend their time groping in the darkness searching for a way out.

Christ offers a different pathway—a pathway to the joy, peace, and brightness of God's love and mercy. When we hear the Holy Spirit calling us to repentance and choose to believe in and receive Jesus Christ as Lord and Savior, we begin to walk with God on the pathway of eternal life. We are justified—made pure, clean, righteous, and just—through the shed blood of Jesus Christ.

God's Word declares that the path of the *just* will become brighter and brighter until the perfect day—the day of Christ's return to earth for His bride.

Webster's New World Dictionary defines *just* as upright (honest and honorable; standing vertical) and righteous (doing what is right; acting in a just, upright manner). In the weakness of our flesh, we could never hope to become just; but through the shed blood of Jesus Christ we have been made just—just as if we had never sinned.

We now have the daily opportunity to shine brighter and brighter for the Lord. By doing so, we dispel darkness and light the way for others to find Christ.

Father, help me walk in a way that I will light the path leading others to You. Thank You for being the shining light in my life.

Meet the Authors

M. L. Anderson is a contributing writer for *Bookstore Journal, Aspiring Retail,* and *Retailing Resources* magazines. His stories appear in *American Moments, Stepping Stones, The Desk in the Attic,* and *No Small Miracles* anthology books. Mike has served as president of the Christian Authors Guild and is currently the CAG Membership Director.

Diana J. Baker is a columnist and Associate Editor of *Christian Living* magazine. Her articles and stories have appeared in *Focus on the Family* publications and in anthology books. Diana has been a member of the Christian Authors Guild for eight years, serving as hospitality chairman, historian, president, and special projects director.

Pam I. Barnes works at Kennesaw State University. She has taught "The Person behind the Pen," a series of classes about famous authors. Her writing interests include Christian fiction and poetry. Pam has a B.S degree in Marketing from Jacksonville State University. She is the Christian Authors Guild 2008 Conference Director.

Marcus Beavers, former chaplain of the Christian Authors Guild, has written over 20 mysteries and hopes to "create a better mouse trap" as a mystery writer. His stories appear in *Stepping Stones, The Desk in the Attic,* and *No Small Miracles* anthologies. He enjoys attending the Blue Ridge Mountains Christian Writers Conference.

Judy Becker, vice president of the Christian Authors Guild for 2006-2007, writes mostly prophecy. WinePress Publishing published her book, *Rightly Dividing the Book of Revelation,* in 2004, while Tate Publishing will publish her fictional work, *The Beginning of the End,* in 2008. Judy's other articles and books await acceptance.

Heartfelt Inspirations

Mildred McDonald-Carter is one of the newer members of the Christian Authors Guild. She loves to write poetry and especially enjoys using scriptures from the Bible in her poems. Mildred, a wife and mother of five, is retired from the Internal Revenue Service and currently works as a sales associate.

Cheryl Anderson Davis is a history buff with two historical novels in print. The Revolutionary War is the setting of *Hope is Constant*, which won Trebel Heart Books' Best Historical Book Award. Her novel, *Southern Complications*, published by Whiskey Creek Press, is a story of the Reconstruction Era in Georgia.

Joan Duvall enjoys writing stories about her personal experiences with God and about the things she observes in everyday life. Joan's goal is to help her readers perceive God with a more far-reaching way of thinking. She shares that through faith we can learn that God is closer than we imagine.

Charlene Elder enjoys writing fiction short stories as well as poetry and non-fiction articles. Charlene has contributed as writer/co-editor of a nation-wide ministry newsletter, *The Salt Shaker*. She has served as CAG's secretary and is currently CAG's chaplain. She writes for CAG's newsletter, *The* Wave, and co-edits it with her husband, Jack.

Jack G. Elder, a former pastor and a freelance writer from Woodstock, Georgia, enjoys writing historical fiction. Jack has served as treasurer of the Christian Authors Guild and is currently the editor of the CAG newsletter, *The WAVE*. His memoirs and stories have appeared in CAG anthology books.

Robert W. Ellis has authored dialogue for nine Christmas pageants, a number of dramatic sketches, and *The Journey*, a three-act evangelical play. He has also been published by the National Drama Service. His memoirs and stories have been published in three CAG anthologies. Robert and his wife, Nanci, live Marietta, Georgia.

Margaret Fagre writes devotions as well as a weekly study guide for a Bible study group. Peggy has been an active member of the Christian Authors Guild for several years. She and Richard, her husband of forty-five years, make their home in Acworth, Georgia.

Louise Flanders worked for ten years as a procedures writer and now enjoys writing Christian articles and devotionals. She is currently the Christian Authors Guild Secretary and has attended two CAG writer's conferences. Louise participates in a non-fiction critique group and has recently completed her first non-fiction book.

Meet the Authors

Dorothy Frassetto lives in Canton, Georgia with her husband, Jim. Dorothy writes poetry and has been published in *Twilight Musings*. She has published one biography, *Kitchen, Children, Church,* and has two short stories in *Stepping Stones*, a book of collected memoirs. She is currently working on another biography.

Bonnie Greenwood Grant is a writer and a gifted wood carver. Bonnie carved three animals for the endangered species carousel at the Chattanooga Zoo. She shares her talents in her new book, *Carving Carousel Animals*. Bonnie uses humor to illustrate Christian concepts in her novels, *Run for Your Life* and *Home Coming*.

Toni Kiriakopoulos, a new member of the Christian Authors Guild, is embarking on her writing career at the age of 68. She has written a book about her son entitled, *Child of My Heart*. She enjoys writing short stories and entering writing contests.

Bill Larmore, who recently celebrated his 90th birthday and is CAG's oldest member, writes poetry, short stories, and magazine articles. He has been published in earlier CAG books, poetry anthologies—including the 2006 and 2007 Kennesaw State University "Poetry of the Golden Generation" books—and in Tyndale House Devotionals.

Burl McCosh has spent sixteen years doing technical writing in the electric power industry and is a freelance writer for *Christian Living* magazine. He writes gospel songs and poetry, typically with a Christian living theme. Burl's primary writing purpose is to express ideas and entertain in a clean and wholesome fashion.

Adrienne A. Nelson holds a B.A. degree in English from Kennesaw State University having studied English Literature and Poetry. In college she wrote for *The Sentinel* newspaper and was published in *Share* Magazine. She has worked at the University of Georgia Library.

Gail Pallotta has published articles and poems in local, regional, and national publications. Author of *Now Is The Time*, Gail was the 2004 Atlanta Writer of the Year for the American Christian Writers Association. Her Christian e-book, *Love Turns the Tide*, will come out on Awe-Struck E-Books in 2009.

June Parks, librarian for the Christian Authors Guild, says she writes because she must. My grandchildren must hear about my safe, easy, citified childhood, my precious Daddy, my up-by-her-bootstraps Mom, and my wonderful husband. June writes memoirs about family members because she believes "a good life needs to be chronicled."

Heartfelt Inspirations

Judy Parrott combines her love for motorcycle riding and people with her love for writing. She enjoys writing true miracle stories about bikers and other people. Judy and her husband, Roger, live in Cumming, Georgia when they are not adventuring around the countryside looking for stories for Judy to write.

Patty Rocco enjoys writing devotionals and Bible studies for her church. She also writes fiction. One of her short stories won 2nd place in the 2007 Christian Authors Guild Fiction Writing Contest. Patty and her husband, John, reside in the Atlanta area.

Susan M. Schulz, a Bible teacher, writer, wife, and mother of three, lives in Woodstock, Georgia. Susan has been published in several anthology books. Her deep passion to encourage the children of God to hear His magnificent voice through prayer and Bible study has birthed her blog spot, Listening Hearts Ministry.

Cynthia L. Simmons has served as conference director, chaplain and president of the Christian Authors Guild. Her work has appeared in the CAG anthologies, *Chattanooga Times Free Press*, *NATHHAN NEWS*, *Chattanooga Regional Historical Journal*, and *Georgia Right to Life News*. *Struggles and Triumphs*, her first book, was published in 2008.

Brenda Thompson Ward has served as librarian and hospitality chairman for the Christian Authors Guild. Her memoirs and stories appear in *Stepping Stones*, *The Desk in the Attic*, and *No Small Miracles* anthologies. Brenda published her first novel in 2000. When she is not writing she enjoys teaching ladies' Bible studies.

Susan M. Watkins, a native Chicagoan, won her first writing contest at age eleven. Previously a writer for The Christian Broadcasting Network's television program, *The 700 Club*, Susan has more recently been featured in *The One Year Life Verse Devotional*, The Atlanta-Journal Constitution, writing competitions, and literary and financial newsletters.

To order additional copies of this title:
Please visit our Web site at
www.pleasantwordbooks.com

If you enjoyed this quality custom-published book,
drop by our Web site for more books and information.

www.winepressgroup.com
"Your partner in custom publishing."

Printed in the United States
138342LV00002B/1/P